Daring to Hope

THE AZRIELI SERIES OF HOLOCAUST SURVIVOR MEMOIRS: PUBLISHED TITLES

ENGLISH TITLES

William Tannenzapf, *Memories from the Abyss/* Renate Krakauer, *But I Had a Happy Childhood*
Elsa Thon, *If Only It Were Fiction*
Agnes Tomasov, *From Generation to Generation*

Joseph Tomasov, *From Loss to Liberation*
Sam Weisberg, *Carry the Torch/* Johnny Jablon, *A Lasting Legacy*
Leslie Vertes, *Alone in the Storm*
Anka Voticky, *Knocking on Every Door*

TITRES FRANÇAIS

Judy Abrams, *Retenue par un fil/* Eva Felsenburg Marx, *Une question de chance*
Molly Applebaum, *Les Mots enfouis: Le Journal de Molly Applebaum*
Claire Baum, *Le Colis caché*
Bronia et Joseph Beker, *Plus forts que le malheur*
Max Bornstein, *Citoyen de nulle part*
Tommy Dick, *Objectif: survivre*
Marian Domanski, *Traqué*
John Freund, *La Fin du printemps*
Myrna Goldenberg (Éditrice), *Un combat singulier: Femmes dans la tourmente de l'Holocauste*
René Goldman, *Une enfance à la dérive*
Anna Molnár Hegedűs, *Pendant la saison des lilas*
Helena Jockel, *Nous chantions en sourdine*
Michael Kutz, *Si, par miracle*
Nate Leipciger, *Le Poids de la liberté*
Alex Levin, *Étoile jaune, étoile rouge*
Fred Mann, *Un terrible revers de fortune*
Michael Mason, *Au fil d'un nom*

Leslie Meisels, *Soudains, les ténèbres*
Muguette Myers, *Les Lieux du courage*
Arthur Ney, *L'Heure W*
Felix Opatowski, *L'Antichambre de l'enfer*
Marguerite Élias Quddus, *Cachée*
Henia Reinhartz, *Fragments de ma vie*
Betty Rich, *Seule au monde*
Paul-Henri Rips, *Matricule E/96*
Steve Rotschild, *Sur les traces du passé*
Kitty Salsberg et Ellen Foster, *Unies dans l'épreuve*
Zuzana Sermer, *Trousse de survie*
Rachel Shtibel, *Le Violon/* Adam Shtibel, *Témoignage d'un enfant*
George Stern, *Une jeunesse perdue*
Willie Sterner, *Les Ombres du passé*
Ann Szedlecki, *L'Album de ma vie*
William Tannenzapf, *Souvenirs de l'abîme/* Renate Krakauer, *Le Bonheur de l'innocence*
Elsa Thon, *Que renaisse demain*
Agnes Tomasov, *De génération en génération*
Leslie Vertes, *Seul dans la tourmente*
Anka Voticky, *Frapper à toutes les portes*

Daring to Hope

Rachel Lisogurski and Chana Broder

THE AZRIELI FOUNDATION · www.azrielifoundation.org

Epigraph on page 4 from *The Jewish Study Bible: Jewish Publication Society Tanakh*, Translation by Adele Berlin and Marc Zvi Brettler, 2003.

Cover and book design by Mark Goldstein
Map on page xxxi by Deborah Crowle
Family Tree on page xxxii–xxxiii by Keaton Taylor
Endpaper maps by Martin Gilbert

LIBRARY AND ARCHIVES CANADA CATALOGUING IN PUBLICATION

Daring to Hope/Rachel Lisogurski and Chana Broder

Lisogurski, Rachel, 1911–1998 author. Broder, Chana, 1938– author.
Azrieli Foundation, publisher.
Azrieli series of Holocaust survivor memoirs. Series XII
Includes bibliographical references and index.
Canadiana 20200291475 · ISBN 9781988065588 (softcover) · 8 7 6 5 4 3 2 1

LCSH: Lisogurski, Rachel, 1911–1998 LCSH: Broder, Chana, 1938– LCSH: Holocaust, Jewish (1939-1945) — Poland — Siemiatycze — Personal narratives. LCSH: Jews — Poland — Siemiatycze — Biography. LCSH: Holocaust survivors — Poland — Siemiatycze — Biography. LCSH: Holocaust survivors — Canada — Biography. LCGFT: Autobiographies.

LCC DS134.7 .L57 2020 DDC 940.53/18092271—DC23

MIX
Paper from
responsible sources
FSC
www.fsc.org   FSC® C004191

PRINTED IN CANADA

The Azrieli Foundation's Holocaust Survivor Memoirs Program

Naomi Azrieli, Publisher

Jody Spiegel, Program Director
Arielle Berger, Managing Editor
Catherine Person, French Translations, Manager and Editor
Matt Carrington, Editor
Devora Levin, Editor and Special Projects Coordinator
Elin Beaumont, Community and Education Initiatives
Stephanie Corazza, Academic and Education Initiatives
Marc-Olivier Cloutier, School and Education Initiatives
Elizabeth Banks, Digital Asset Curator and Archivist
Catherine Quintal, Digital Communications Assistant

Mark Goldstein, Art Director
Bruno Paradis, Layout, French-Language Editions

Contents

Series Preface:
In their own words. . .

In telling these stories, the writers have liberated themselves. For so many years we did not speak about it, even when we became free people living in a free society. Now, when at last we are writing about what happened to us in this dark period of history, knowing that our stories will be read and live on, it is possible for us to feel truly free. These unique historical documents put a face on what was lost, and allow readers to grasp the enormity of what happened to six million Jews — one story at a time.

    David J. Azrieli, C.M., C.Q., M.Arch
    Holocaust survivor and founder, The Azrieli Foundation

Since the end of World War II, approximately 40,000 Jewish Holocaust survivors have immigrated to Canada. Who they are, where they came from, what they experienced and how they built new lives for themselves and their families are important parts of our Canadian heritage. The Azrieli Foundation's Holocaust Survivor Memoirs Program was established in 2005 to preserve and share the memoirs written by those who survived the twentieth-century Nazi genocide of the Jews of Europe and later made their way to Canada. The memoirs encourage readers to engage thoughtfully and critically with the complexities of the Holocaust and to create meaningful connections with the lives of survivors.

Millions of individual stories are lost to us forever. By preserving the stories written by survivors and making them widely available to a broad audience, the Azrieli Foundation's Holocaust Survivor Memoirs Program seeks to sustain the memory of all those who perished at the hands of hatred, abetted by indifference and apathy. The personal accounts of those who survived against all odds are as different as the people who wrote them, but all demonstrate the courage, strength, wit and luck that it took to prevail and survive in such terrible adversity. The memoirs are also moving tributes to people — strangers and friends — who risked their lives to help others, and who, through acts of kindness and decency in the darkest of moments, frequently helped the persecuted maintain faith in humanity and courage to endure. These accounts offer inspiration to all, as does the survivors' desire to share their experiences so that new generations can learn from them.

The Holocaust Survivor Memoirs Program collects, archives and publishes select survivor memoirs and makes the print editions available free of charge to educational institutions and Holocaust-education programs across Canada. They are also available for sale online to the general public. All revenues to the Azrieli Foundation from the sales of the Azrieli Series of Holocaust Survivor Memoirs go toward the publishing and educational work of the memoirs program.

⁓

The Azrieli Foundation would like to express appreciation to the following people for their invaluable efforts in producing this book: Doris Bergen, Mark Duffus (Maracle Inc.), Barb Feldman, Farla Klaiman, Susan Roitman, Stephen Ullstrom, and Margie Wolfe & Emma Rodgers of Second Story Press.

Chana Broder wishes to thank Arielle Berger and the entire staff at the Azrieli Foundation, whose efforts brought this book to light.

About the Glossary

The following memoir contains a number of terms, concepts and historical references that may be unfamiliar to the reader. For example, the words Pan and Panie preceding Polish names are male and female honorifics, terms of respect used in Poland, Ukraine and elsewhere. English translations of other foreign-language words and terms have been added, as have parentheses for the names of present-day towns and cities. For general information on major organizations, significant historical events and people, geographical locations, religious and cultural terms, and foreign-language words and expressions that will help give context and background to the events described in the text, please see the glossary beginning on page 173.

Introduction

Grodzisk, the hometown of Rachel Lisogurski (née Kejles), is a small village in what is now eastern Poland, in the district of Bielsk Podlaski, around one hundred and fifty kilometres from Warsaw. In 1921, out of 274 inhabitants in Grodzisk, there were 34 Jews (about 13 per cent of the population), as well as 89 Catholics and 151 Eastern Orthodox. Rachel's brother Shieh (Yehoshua) Kejles had a dairy in Grodzisk, and her parents, Rivka and Ephraim Kejles, had a shop. Rachel married Abraham Lisogurski and lived in his hometown of Siemiatycze (twenty kilometres from Grodzisk). In 1938, their only daughter, Chana, was born.

Grodzisk and Siemiatycze are located in the historical region called Podlasie, which was a melting pot of intermingled and competing Polish, Russian and Lithuanian influences. In the late sixteenth century, petty nobility — impoverished small landowners — began to settle there, encouraged by the dukes in the neighbouring territory of Mazovia who sought to colonize the region. Before long, Lithuanian dukes began colonization of the land from the east, settling peasants of Russian origin there. These types of settlements, combined with invasions, wars and the repeated redrawing of borders, shaped the unique social and national structure of the region: Polish Roman Catholics and impoverished nobility dwelled in both petty-nobility villages and peasant villages within the rural populations around the Eastern Orthodox and Greek Catholic churches.

The first Jews came to Siemiatycze from Lithuania in 1582, brought by the town's owners in order to stimulate the town economically. By 1667, the Jewish community was officially established, and the surviving synagogue dates to 1797. In the eighteenth century, Siemiatycze became the largest town in the Białystok region, and it was inhabited by Poles, Ruthenians and Jews. At the end of the nineteenth century, there were about 4,600 Jews, approximately 75 per cent of the population, living in Siemiatycze.[1] According to the 1921 census, 65 per cent of the town's 6,000 inhabitants were Jews, 25 per cent were Catholics, and 9 per cent were Eastern Orthodox.

Some Jews in Siemiatycze worked in crafts and industry, but their main occupations were in the trade of forest products and grain. In 1890, Hersz Belkes set up the first of the town's tile factories, using the local clay. Siemiatycze then became famous for its production of these tiles from local clay. By the interwar period there were over fifteen tile shops in Siemiatycze and its surroundings, most of which were owned by Jews. One of the most modern factories was the Aron Dajcz (Deitsch) tile factory, whose tiles were awarded a gold medal at the international industrial exhibition in Paris in 1906. The factory was nationalized after the war and produced tiles until the 1990s. The remains of the factory buildings have now turned to ruins.

After Poland regained its independence in 1918, the process of Jewish emancipation in the country accelerated. Despite the increase in discrimination over the years, Jewish social, political and cultural life began to flourish. Thriving youth organizations and movements, together with political parties expressing all kinds of views, provided reinforcement for emancipation tendencies and spurred changes in the traditional structure and functions of the shtetl.

Several modern Jewish schools played a major role in local cultural life. The largest of these schools, the Kadimah Hebrew school,

---

1   For more information on demographics in Siemiatycze, see https://sztetl.org.pl/en/towns/s/833-siemiatycze/96-local-history/67748-local-history.

fostered numerous pioneers (*chalutzim*) who intended to build their homeland in British Mandate Palestine. Many other Jewish schools operated in town, as well as theatrical groups, orchestras, choirs, sports clubs and libraries. The Zionist movement was especially strong among Jews in Siemiatycze.

In the second half of the 1930s, Podlasie, like the rest of Poland, witnessed the rise of antisemitic sentiments. Rachel's parents, Rivka and Ephraim, closed their business and moved to Warsaw when their store was picketed by their neighbours. The worldwide economic crisis also deepened, which caused an even more complicated situation for Jews in Poland before the outbreak of World War II. At the same time, emigration was becoming more and more difficult, and it was not easy for Jews to escape the increasing antisemitism in Europe.

~

On September 1, 1939, Nazi Germany attacked Poland, and on September 11, they captured Siemiatycze. The German soldiers locked several dozen Jews in the synagogue and threatened to kill them if even one German soldier were to die.

According to the agreements of the pact made between Germany and the Soviet Union, German troops withdrew and the Red Army moved into Poland from the east on September 17. The change in the occupying power came as a relief for Jews in the area. It was believed that the threat of physical violence, persecution and terror that the Nazi occupation would have brought was replaced by a political system promising equality and the absence of antisemitism.

After the rigged elections of October 22, 1939,[2] the Soviet borders moved westward, swallowing more than a half of the lands of the Second Polish Republic. Siemiatycze became part of so-called

---

2 Elections to the People's Assemblies of Western Ukraine and Western Belorussia, held with a view to legitimizing the Soviet occupation of Poland's eastern territories that were annexed to the Soviet Union in the autumn of 1939.

Western Belorussia. Before the outbreak of the war, there had been about 4,300 Jews residing in Siemiatycze, and their number probably increased by more than 3,000 as refugees from the German-occupied part of Poland fled east with the onset of the occupation.

The Jewish community under Soviet rule underwent disintegration: the elites had been decimated, with political leaders and activists arrested or deported to Siberia along with local luminaries and the more affluent. Sometimes the arrests happened with the participation of resident supporters of the new order. Nonetheless, very few local Jews found a position within the new system of power. The Soviets had more confidence in their own apparatchiks, and it was they who formed the core of the new regime.

Among the miseries of the Soviet system were shortages of basic food and clothing; forced lodging of Soviet officials; political and religious repressions; the constant threat of the secret police, the NKVD; and surveillance, denunciations and arrests. Saturday was no longer a day of rest for the Jewish community, and loss of income undermined the existence of all locally funded Jewish institutions such as synagogues, study halls, schools, orphanages and nursing homes. The character of Jewish and Hebrew schools had to change, as lessons in Russian were now mandatory.

The disintegration of the social infrastructure was accompanied by widespread transferring of ownership. Small-shop owners and merchants — members of what the Soviet leadership considered "the owners' class" — were listed among the ideological enemies of the system. As part of the nationalization process, Jews, along with the rest of the citizens, were dispossessed of their factories, workshops and stores, which were in turn transformed into cooperatives, following the Soviet model. During the occupation, the Soviets deported more than 300,000 Polish citizens, including about 80,000 Jews, among them at least several dozen Jews from Siemiatycze, to the northern parts of the USSR's Asian republics. Paradoxically, a large number of those deported escaped the Holocaust at the hands of the Germans.

Operation Barbarossa, the Third Reich's invasion of the Soviet Union, commenced on June 22, 1941. The German army swiftly moved east, and on June 23 they arrived in Siemiatycze. After twenty-one months under Soviet rule, Siemiatycze returned to German rule, where it would remain for the next three years. The Soviet authorities left behind a land thrown into chaos, its inhabitants exhausted, insecure and confused.

In the summer of 1941, during the "interregnum period," when there was a power vacuum after the Red Army pulled out, several anti-semitic riots broke out in towns and villages in the Podlasie region. The most infamous and bloody events took place in the town of Jedwabne, in the Łomża region, where other pogroms occurred. The roots of the anti-Jewish riots were in pre-war antisemitism that was amplified during the Soviet occupation by the stereotypes of Jews as communists, combined with the antisemitism reinforced by the Germans.

Rachel Lisogurski's brother Shieh Kejles stated in his post-war testimony that in Siemiatycze, on July 10, after a few days of mounting tension:

Poles, on their own initiative, gathered all Jews [...] and ordered them to dismantle a Lenin monument. The Jews had to wrap the dismantled pieces up in sheets and carry them to the cemetery, where they were forced to make a loud cry. The road to the cemetery led past the river, and when the Jews were crossing the bridge, they were pushed off it into water. In the process of throwing the Jews off the bridge into the water, one Jew died when his head struck a pillar of the bridge.[3]

Siemiatycze was now part of the newly established administrative area called the Bezirk (District) Białystok. Its civil administration was

---

3 Jewish Historical Institute, testimony of Jehoszua (Yehoshua) Kajles (Kejles) 301/1463.

headed by Erich Koch, *Gauleiter* (District Leader) and *Oberpräsident* (Senior President) of East Prussia, who reported directly to Adolf Hitler. German police authorities were also established: State Police and the Criminal Police, as well as the Security Police and Order Police, had branches in Białystok.

The German authorities soon introduced new rules for life under the occupation, among them special anti-Jewish regulations. One of the earliest regulations required Jews to wear identifying armbands. The Germans also imposed heavy forced contributions on the Jews, deciding amounts arbitrarily and demanding to be paid repeatedly, often under threat of mass murder. Judenräte (Jewish councils), as well as Jewish police forces, were established in all municipalities, including Siemiatycze. They administered the day-to-day affairs of Jewish communities, at least in theory. First and foremost, the Jewish councils had to carry out German orders. The Judenrat in Siemiatycze was headed by Israel Rosencwajg (Rosenzweig), who was a neighbour of Rachel Lisogurski's; they lived in the same house in the ghetto, and he was later in hiding with Rachel for a short time after escaping from the ghetto.

From the very beginning of the German occupation, Jews in Siemiatycze, like Jews everywhere in occupied Poland, were rounded up on the streets and forced to perform various jobs, which usually resulted in humiliations and beatings. When compulsory labour was officially introduced for men aged eighteen to sixty, the Jews were required to perform a variety of tasks: cleaning streets, working at the train station and demolishing tombstones in the cemetery.

The Siemiatycze ghetto was established at the beginning of August 1942, three months before the liquidation of Jews in the whole region. The ghetto was bordered by Górna, Wysoka, Słowiczyńska and Koszarowa Streets and was surrounded with a high barbed-wire fence. More than 6,000 people were locked in it, including the Kejles and Lisogurski families.

The liquidation of the ghetto in Siemiatycze, as well as the ghettos of the entire district, excluding those in Białystok and Prużana, began on November 2, 1942. Early in the morning, the German gendarmerie and police surrounded all the ghettos in the county. The deportations were carried out by the combined forces of the gendarmerie and auxiliary police, as well as by supplementary forces: Wehrmacht soldiers, Polish and Ukrainian guards, and even German civilian officials. Between November 2 and 15, the Jews from the entire Bielsk County were gradually transported to the Treblinka death camp, with those from smaller localities — Drohiczyn, Grodzisk and Mielnik — concentrated first in the ghettos in Bielsk Podlaski and Siemiatycze.

Jews were allowed to take only their hand luggage and were told that "they would be taken to another place, or that they were going to the Black Sea or the Caucasus."[4] The deportation was accompanied by screams and beatings, which intensified the general chaos and panic. Many Jews were killed that day: in Siemiatycze about 150 people were killed while trying to escape from the ghetto, which was surrounded by German, Ukrainian and Polish policemen.

Some Jews managed to escape the ghetto, and some went into hiding inside the ghetto. Those who remained planned an armed resistance that was supposed to involve setting the ghetto ablaze. It failed, and all the Jews in hiding were caught. The last transport from the Siemiatycze ghetto carried away all members of the Judenrat and the Jewish police.

Mass breakouts from ghettos were characteristic for Bielsk County, and there were large groups that managed to escape from a few ghettos. Certainly, the proximity of forests, combined with awareness of what the deportation (alluded to as "resettlement") meant, made the decision to escape easier. Sometimes, encouragement came from the ghetto's authorities. The deputy chairman of the Siemiatycze Judenrat, Kruszewski, allegedly urged Jews to escape by saying, "Children, save yourselves, let the Lord deliver you."[5]

---

4 Testimony of Rabbi Halperin, AYV, M11/50.
5 Jewish Historical Institute, testimony of Kalman Krawiec 301/4086.

Rarely were the escapes adequately prepared for, and even if they were planned, in the end, they were executed among the chaos and panic of deportation. Many attempts ended in failure. Some escapees came back to the ghetto disheartened by the futile search for people who would help them; some returned because they didn't want to be separated from their families. Survivor Chaim Marmur recollects in the Siemiatycze Yizkor (memorial) book[6] that about sixty escapees from the Siemiatycze ghetto returned after just a few days as they had been unable to find any shelter. Others who had been hiding in the nearby forest for two weeks gave up and turned themselves over to the police, who murdered them in the Jewish cemetery.

Searching for rescue outside the ghetto, among the local inhabitants, was not easy. People were afraid to help because the punishment for helping the Jews was death. The refusal to help was understandable in the context of the occupation-time reality and although perhaps we cannot say that everyone was obliged to help, we can nonetheless assess damaging attitudes toward Jews.

While the escapees were trying to size up the situation, identify opportunities and work out strategies, the abandoned ghettos were being stripped of any valuables left behind and combed in search of Jews in hiding. Unfortunately, for Jews in hiding, robbery, denunciations and murder were everyday experiences. For some neighbours, the Jews' plight turned out to be an opportunity for swift enrichment. Greed and a lack of moral scruples played a part in preying on the Jews. The opportunities to deceive and exploit were considerable, and tempting because they could be carried out practically with impunity.

---

6 E. Tash, editor, *Kehilat Semyatitch* (The Community of Semyatitch). (Tel Aviv: Association of Former Residents of Semiatich in Israel and the Diaspora, 1965), https://www.jewishgen.org/yizkor/siemiatycze1/siemiatycze1.html.

An incomparably greater risk was taken when helping Jews. Helping meant risking one's life whereas denunciation could bring rewards — sometimes a kilogram of sugar, some vodka or cigarettes and sometimes the murdered person's belongings. Factors that played a key role in denunciations of Jews were, on the one hand, fear and the shrewd fear management on the part of the Germans and, on the other, the concurrence of evil and coincidence, when Jews, by pure chance, found themselves in the wrong place at the wrong time. There was no shortage of malice.

Survival depended on the ability to avoid danger, whether from Germans or Poles; the resources in one's possession (the ability to pay for help); and luck — the chance of finding people ready to risk their own safety to help. For Jews who were seeking refuge, their resources, determination or will to live could only influence their survival to a small degree. Evil, in the form of fear, hate or greed, had more power here. Most attempts to survive, even if initially successful, ended with death.

The Jews from Siemiatycze and the surrounding area who survived did so on gentiles' farms and in partisan detachments operating in the local forests. At the end of 1942, Soviet partisan units were operating in the county, and detachments of Polish partisans were being formed. Jewish partisans from Drohiczyn, Brańsk and Siemiatycze had at first belonged to "survival groups" of escapees from different ghettos before they gradually became partisans. These self-defense groups not only fought for their own survival but — being armed — actively defended the Jews hiding nearby and punished those who handed them over to the Germans. They also carried out sabotage operations.

One of the most active groups in the vicinity of Siemiatycze was led by Hershl (Herschel) Shabbes. After buying one pistol, the group began to plan more intensive activity against the peasants who were informing on or killing Jews, as recorded in the Siemiatycze Yizkor book:

A warning was issued to the district peasants that revenge would be taken for betraying a Jew to the Germans. And the Semiatych Jews soon proved that they would follow through. They learned that a peasant had caught Velvl Shoshkes, Israel Kravitz's uncle, and chained him to his cart and taken him to the Gestapo, where he was shot. Several days later, the peasant was killed. This was the first act of vengeance, but not the last.[7]

∽

In *Daring to Hope*, Rachel Lisogurski's memories focus on the period of hiding after she and her family escaped from the ghetto, or, more accurately, how much effort, courage and determination she put into saving her family. Deciding to escape was not easy — it meant opposing the group instinct, the general tendency to "be together with everyone." And Rachel understood what displacement meant. When Rachel decided to escape from the ghetto with her husband and their four-year-old daughter, she carefully considered how to implement her plan. She writes, "The question of where I would hide didn't stop hammering in my head. How will we hide? What will I do? And every time I thought about it, I reached the same decision: I'll try; I have nothing to lose. And I did have some hope. I knew so many gentiles. Maybe one of them would help us." The people from whom she expected help — a friend from school, a neighbour to whom they gave their belongings for safekeeping — failed them. They refused to help, threw Rachel and her family out of their homes and stole from them. Contrary to Rachel's expectations, they were helped by people who were practically strangers.

Rachel Lisogurski, like many escapees from ghettos in the area, initially found herself in the forest with a large group of other Jews.

---

7 N.N., *Semiatych – Its Growth and Destruction*, translated by Adah B. Fogel, http://www.jewishgen.org/yizkor/siemiatycze1/sie500.html.

After a few days, the group divided into smaller family-based groups, and each one attempted to find an anchoring point, a base, if only temporarily. Most often, a small group could find a place for the night and some provisions to carry them through a few days, a week, or sometimes longer.

The Lisogurski family followed this pattern: wandering, interspersed with stopovers in the woods, encounters (often chance encounters) with other Jews as they looked for the next point of anchor — and so on. Threats periodically disrupted this pattern — accidents, betrayals, a robbery, a denunciation and a lucky escape. Rachel writes many moving scenes of begging for help, of humiliation, of fear and of ruthless treatment of Jews by people with whom they had been neighbours for years. After several months of hiding, some people she either knew or were related to were discovered, denounced and killed by the Germans. News about these murders travelled fast, and fear and anxiety grew.

Among the many poignant situations described in the memoir is one where the author's mother, who has been shot in the shoulder, crawls out from under the corpses of fourteen other Jews killed by the Germans, including her own husband. No wonder that after such an experience she would often speak to herself. "What had happened to the Germans? What had gotten into them?" she would ponder. We are still looking for an answer to this question today.

Over the course of time, the Jews gained experience, and their expertise in hiding grew. Rachel knew how to talk to Poles, and her knowledge of human nature, as well as her courage, were extraordinary and impressive. Her words to one farmer, Wojtkowski, who refused to help the Lisogurski family, are very moving:

If only you would help us a little. I don't mean you personally, but all you Poles, our neighbours, people we went to school with, whom we saw every day, did business with. Now everybody turns their backs on us.

We were born here; we grew up together. Now you people are helping the Germans kill us. [...] Poland, who herself was in slavery for more than a hundred years under the Russian Tsar, is now selling herself for the price of Jewish lives. Who will pay for the crimes committed in the twentieth century?

Rachel and her family, after wandering for some time, found refuge in Klemens's barn for several months. It is worth noting how important belongings were for survival — there was poverty in the countryside that is hard to imagine today, and greed proved to be one of the most important motivations for help, and sometimes betrayal. Rachel wrote, "Who could figure these people out? When they came for our things, they were kind and sweet as honey. But how quickly they showed themselves to be snakes and murderers! Without our possessions we had nothing to offer, and pity was very hard to find."

The Lisogurski family stayed at Klemens's farm until May 1943, paying him with possessions that they recovered, with difficulty, from the people who were holding them for safekeeping. Other Jews, family and friends from Siemiatycze, were also hiding in the area. They all tried to keep in touch and help each other, sharing the items they had managed to hide and bury, which now enabled them to pay for hiding.

After leaving Klemens's farm, the Lisogurskis found shelter for a few weeks with the Boguszewski family, where Rachel and her mother earned their living knitting. They then found a place with the Krynski family in the village of Morze. The Krynski family had agreed to take them for two weeks but then didn't have the heart to throw them out. They were deeply religious people who turned out to be exceptionally empathic and grateful. Pan Krynski said to Rachel:

I was a prisoner in Germany during World War I, and I know what hunger means. You are facing death without ever having committed a crime. Who should we help? The Germans who grabbed our country and are destroying it? Or you? You don't know me, but after I got out of the German prison, I was poor, and your father used to lend me salt and fuel.

The Lisogurskis had run out of items to pay with, but the Krynski family, in contrast to the previous families they had found shelter with, did not demand anything. The Krynskis were so poor that they didn't have enough potatoes to feed their pigs, but they would give what little they had put aside for their animals to the family instead. They built a hiding place under the floor of the barn (which later proved valuable in a critical situation), and members of their family who were hiding in the area brought them food so they would not starve. During the year of hiding with the Krynski family, there were moments of crisis, including a dramatic attack by the Polish national underground, who beat Krynski and looked for hidden Jews.

The Red Army entered the region of Siemiatycze in late July 1944, liberating towns one after the other. On August 23, 1944, the County National Council in Bielsk Podlaski was formed, and the creation of the new socialist system under Moscow's supervision had begun. The anti-Communist underground put up an armed resistance to the new regime, and chaos and violence ruled Bielsk County throughout the first years after the war. The new central administration's reach did not extend there, and the local authorities were losing the battle with the armed underground and common bandits.

The Jews who had survived, now free, directed their first steps toward their hometowns but were by no means welcomed there. The Lisogurskis returned to Siemiatycze, but the gentile people who were living in their home did not want to let them in. The Jews had new dangers to face, the sources of which can be traced to three main roots: greed related to appropriated Jewish property, moral decay (that manifested itself in widespread banditry), and antisemitism founded on stereotypes, both old and new.

xxviii DARING TO HOPE

In Siemiatycze, on December 13, 1944, a Jewish man named Brukier was attacked by the Polish underground; on January 5, 1945, a Jewish miller, Ben Lev, was attacked.[8]

On April 6, 1945, a battle took place in Siemiatycze: a Polish underground group launched an attack on two buildings inhabited by Jews. A witness to those events, Jankiel Blusztein, recalled:

All Jews, some fifty persons, gathered in the attic [of the house] on Ciechanowiecka Street, and began to fire and throw grenades [...]. The battle lasted for three hours. One woman was killed. By coincidence, several vehicles carrying Soviet soldiers arrived [...] we were saved by this. The next day after this incident, several military cars came and took us to Bielsk.[9]

At that time, the Lisogurskis were already in Białystok. At the end of April 1945, together with Rachel's sister Henia Zoltak and her husband, Israel (Sruleh), and their son, Yehoshua (Shieleh), the Lisogurskis left Poland and travelled through Slovakia, Hungary, Romania and Italy, where they spent close to three years. In 1948, they went to Canada.

~

Rachel Lisogurski is an insightful observer of human nature. In her writing, she analyzes the motivations of her own and others' actions, her wisdom and life experience acting as a catalyst for many deep and important reflections. What distinguishes her memoir from many others is a conscious description of emotions and psychological truths, which allows the reader to understand the horrors experienced during hiding, as well as how much effort, courage and willpower it took to persevere.

---

8 Reports of the Citizens' Militia (Milicja Obywatelska) from Bielsk Podlaski, AIPN Bi, 047/13, t. 1, k. 4. In Rachel Lisogurski's memoir the attack on Lev is approximated as occurring in late 1944.

9 Ibid.

Chana Broder, Rachel's daughter, whose memories are part of the publication and not only complement the family history but also elaborate on their postwar lives, describes the Jews who survived in hiding as feeling like "second-class survivors." Recalling a conversation she had with her mother when Rachel wrote her memoirs in 1967, a time when nobody wanted to publish such testimonies, Chana writes:

Our story was not dramatic enough. We had always felt like second-class survivors — we had not slaved in a concentration camp, we had not smelled the odour of the crematoria smoke, we had not been forced on a death march. We had "only" hidden like mice in holes for twenty months, suffered hunger and cold, feared for our lives every day and night.

Thanks to the memoirs of Rachel Lisogurski and her daughter, Chana Broder, we have a better understanding that hiding is an important part of the history of the Holocaust.

Professor Barbara Engelking
Polish Center of Holocaust Research, Institute of Philosophy and Sociology of the Polish Academy of Sciences
2019

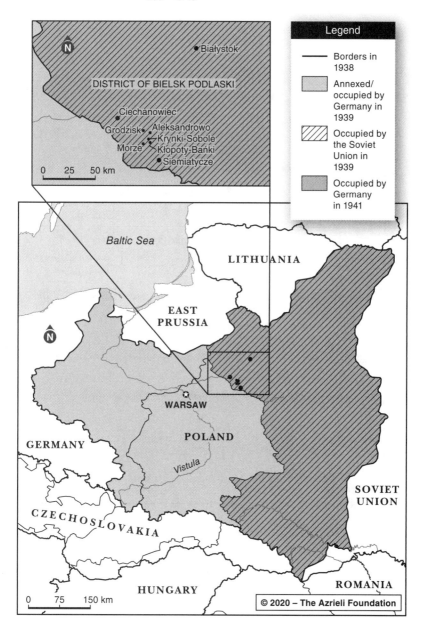

Chana Broder Family Tree

MATERNAL GRANDPARENTS:
Rivka (née Levin) and Ephraim* Kejles (Kalles)

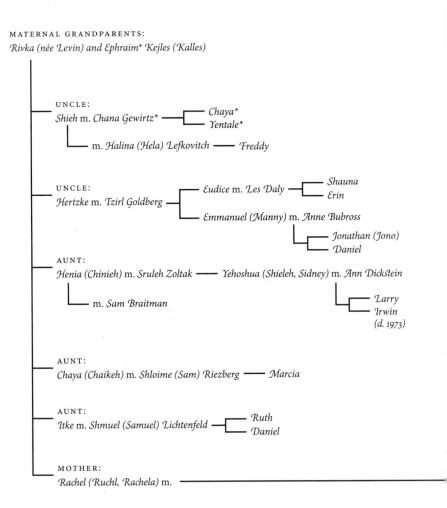

UNCLE:
Shieh m. *Chana Gewirtz** ── *Chaya**
Yentale*

m. *Halina (Hela) Lefkovitch* ──── *Freddy*

UNCLE:
Hertzke m. *Tzirl Goldberg* ── *Eudice* m. *Les Daly* ── *Shauna*
Erin

Emmanuel (Manny) m. *Anne Bubross*

Jonathan (Jono)
Daniel

AUNT:
Henia (Chinieh) m. *Sruleh Zoltak* ──── *Yehoshua (Shieleh, Sidney)* m. *Ann Dickstein*

m. *Sam Braitman*

Larry
Irwin
(d. 1973)

AUNT:
Chaya (Chaikeh) m. *Shloime (Sam) Riezberg* ──── *Marcia*

AUNT:
Itke m. *Shmuel (Samuel) Lichtenfeld* ── *Ruth*
Daniel

MOTHER:
Rachel (Ruchl, Rachela) m. ────────────

PATERNAL GRANDPARENTS:
Shmuel* and Ruchl (née Kachka)* Lisogurski

UNCLE:
Pesach* m. Odel* —— *Two children, names unknown*

AUNT:
Pessia* m. Leibel* —— *Daughter, name unknown**

UNCLE:
Yudel*

UNCLE:
Srulek*

FATHER:
Abraham (Avrumeh, Avrum)

Chana (Chanale) m. *Menashe (Tashie) Broder*
(born 1938)

Pnina m. *Navot Manor* ——┌ *Eitan Avraham*
                            └ *Ohad*

David (Shelly) m. *Carmel Gerstner* ——┌ *Yonatan Avraham*
                                        └ *Mika Rachel*

Shlomit m. *Michal Shahak* ——┌ *Amit*
                               ├ *Alma*
                               └ *Noam Amnon*

**Murdered in
the Holocaust*

Rachel Lisogurski

For my grandchildren and their children and grandchildren and the generations to come.

Panic and pitfall are our lot,
Death and destruction.
My eyes shed streams of water
Over the ruin of my poor people.

Lamentations 3:47–48

Prologue

What a relief! Finally, somebody wants to listen to what I went through during the German occupation of Poland. I think my case was a very unusual one, for I fled from the ghetto with a child of four, who I believe was the youngest person to remain alive from a town of approximately four thousand Jews.

Maybe once I write everything down, I will not have so many nightmares about the war. I also hope to be able to repay all those good people who helped us in one way or another. We only correspond with the last family that hid us, the family that helped us most, and we try our best to show our appreciation for their kindness. But for all the others, the least we can do is remember their names. They should never be forgotten for stretching out helping hands to us. We are everlastingly grateful to them. The Polish people should also be very grateful to that small group for helping us Jews, because these humane beings saved Poland's reputation.

I am not a writer, and I can't make the story more or less exciting. I want only to write down what I remember.

Rachel Lisogurski
Montreal, 1967

The Fear Begins

It was July 1, 1942, when the head of the Judenrat, Mr. Rosenzweig, announced that all the Jews from the town of Semiatych (Siemiatycze)[1] would have to go into the ghetto by the first of August.

The ghetto was to be on the side of the town where most of the factories were located. One of those factories had belonged to Maliniak, who manufactured wooden nails for shoes, another to Belkes, who made tiles and other articles, and yet another to Deitsch, also a tilemaker. There were many smaller factories, too, like Cotler's, and others that had belonged to Jews, whom the Soviets had earlier declared to be bourgeois and sent to toil in Siberia. My own sister, Itke, had been sent to Siberia along with her husband.

The gentiles who lived around the factories would be given our houses, and we were to be given their houses. The houses of the Polish working-class were small, one-family structures with three rooms at the most, and with little gardens. Each small house was to be shared by several Jewish families.

---

1   Siemiatycze, a town in eastern Poland, was pronounced in Yiddish as Semiatych by its Jewish community, which was destroyed by the Nazis during World War II. The authors of this memoir have chosen to preserve their former community's usage. Semiatych will be used throughout the memoir unless referring to the present-day town.

But what was to be done with our furniture? I had less worry than others because I had already been robbed the previous year, when the Germans first occupied Semiatych. A boy who thought that we had not served him properly when he came — without money — to get electrical appliances that we were selling, saw to that. He had seen our furniture (which was new, since I had married only three years earlier) and when the Germans arrived and were collecting furniture for their offices, the first house he brought them to was ours. They had taken everything except the bed.

The really troublesome questions for us were which family to share with and which house to take, if there was going to be a choice. I had a feeling that moving to the ghetto would not be our last persecution at the hands of the Germans. But everybody was so busy figuring out how to exchange furniture for food, gold or dollars that they didn't hear, or want to hear, that things could actually get even worse. So we fooled ourselves into believing that we were going to be transferred somewhere to work. Only later did we realize that the ghetto was really a passport to death.

I kept wondering who would want to live with us, with our little Chanale (Chana), who was not even four years old. But one day, Avrumeh, my husband, announced that he had seen Yetta Weinstein and that she wanted to live with us. I was thrilled. She was a cousin to my sister-in-law Chana and was also one of the most intellectual people in Semiatych. She and her husband had a twelve-year-old boy, Chaim, and nine-year-old twin girls. Our two families would have to live in one room.

My father and mother had been living in Semiatych since the end of 1939, when they had moved from Warsaw. A few weeks after the war broke out in September 1939, their building at Nowiniarska 14 had been bombed. It was right after the Yom Kippur fast, before they had a chance to put a piece of bread in their mouths, that there was an explosion in the lower floor of their building. They had to run immediately with my sister Itke, who was living with them at the time. Not having anything left, they all stayed with my father's sister, Dobcia, in Warsaw for a few weeks, before they started to travel the nearly one hundred and fifty kilometres to Semiatych to join me and my siblings Shieh and Chinieh (Henia). My brother Shieh and his wife, Chana, had two daughters, Chaya, fourteen, and Yentale, ten. My sister Henia and her husband, Sruleh, had an eleven-year-old son, also named Shieh (Yehoshua), whom we called Shieleh.

Avrumeh's parents also lived in Semiatych. Many people knew his father, Shmileh (Shmuel) the tailor. He and Avrumeh's mother, Ruchl, lived in a very big house of their own with their two unmarried sons, Yudel, twenty-three, and Srulek, eighteen. Upstairs in the same house lived their son Pesach and his wife, Odel, and their two boys aged five and three, as well as their daughter, Pessia, and her three-year-old girl. Pessia's husband, Leibel, had been taken "to work" by the Soviets in 1940, and we never heard from him again. In the ghetto, my in-laws had gotten a house for themselves and all the children who had been living with them.

The ghetto was in the part of the town that was called "under the bridge." Two major roads cut through it, so the one ghetto had three separate zones, each surrounded by a wooden fence topped with barbed wire. When it was time to move, Avrumeh came home with the news that Mrs. Rosenzweig, too, had asked him if we wanted to live with them. The Rosenzweigs loved our Chanale very much and so did their eighteen-year-old son, Chazkel, and their thirteen-year-old daughter, Ruzka, who often played with Chanale in their home. Mrs. Rosenzweig used to say, "My children are too big for me to play with! Send up your Chana."

Now we had to decide whom to live with and in which part of the ghetto to settle. Because Mr. Rosenzweig was head of the Judenrat, when his wife asked us to live with them, my first thought was, living with them, I'll have a better house. But mostly I just couldn't refuse them, as that would have been an insult, and who wanted to be on bad terms with the leader of the Judenrat? But I explained to them that my parents would have to come along with us. So we all moved in together — me and Avrumeh and Chanale, my parents, my sister Henia with her family, and the Rosenzweigs. All together we were twelve people in two small rooms and a kitchen. We had a garden where potatoes grew. At the end of the garden stood a barbed-wire fence, and just beyond it were the mountains that surrounded that part of the town.

The first month, we were busy getting our house in order. The Rosenzweigs took one room, Henia and I and our families the other one, and my father and mother slept in the kitchen. My mother assured us that the kitchen suited them very well since they always got up earlier in the morning than the rest of us and were too old to jump over our beds, which were in any case pressed so tightly together that there was no space between them.

In the beginning, we really thought that maybe it was better that we lived in the ghetto. With all of us in one place it was easier for the peasants and farmers to come over to the fence, bringing food to exchange for the items we would offer them. The Germans didn't visit the ghetto too often. All their orders were relayed to the Judenrat, and the Jewish police had to carry them out. Every morning, those forced to work gathered and marched out of the ghetto in an orderly file to the main part of town, from where they were sent to different places to work.

Before all this, we had lived in the centre of the town, in a flat we rented from Chaim the shoemaker, whose nickname was Posladke (Buttocks). My windows faced the market and the "Broom," which is what the middle of the city was called. It was shaped like a square, with stores, maybe a hundred of them, all around it, and on top of the stores were apartments. These had been built more than a hundred years earlier and their walls were stone and very thick. People from Semiatych used to say that this "Broom" had survived through many wars and that even fire couldn't destroy it. But as we would see, they hadn't dreamt of a war like this one.

~

It was June 22, 1941, four in the morning, when the Germans began their attack from the other side of the Bug River. All the big shells fell on the Broom, and then from the airplanes came the bombs. At around three in the afternoon the Broom started to burn, and it burned down totally and completely. It took more than a year for the Jewish workers (everybody who was able to stand on their feet was considered a worker) to clean up all the rubble. I was exempt from work because I had a small child, but I used to go over quite often to ease my conscience, and I saw how hard everyone worked and what happened when a worker fell behind. A Nazi and his dog were always watching, and when one of the workers slowed down, the dog would almost tear him to pieces. From my window I would see how the "dog" on two legs would flick his whip against his shiny boots, satisfied that his four-legged beast had done its work so well.

I tried my best to keep Chanale from seeing all the violence. I wanted her to believe that people were good, but being surrounded by all these scenes, I found it was very hard to tell stories about good people. Once, before the ghetto was established, we got caught violating the curfew, and that incident, too, made me feel that we would be better off living in the ghetto. The curfew meant that we were not allowed to go outside after 5:00 p.m. At the time, my parents were living in an apartment above Henia's, two houses away from ours. I had gone to see them with Chanale, and, as grandparents do, they played with her, especially my father. He laughed so heartily at everything she said, and she, seeing her Zaideh laughing so, tried to make him happy. I forgot the time till it was two minutes past five. When I grabbed Chanale and rushed out the door, I saw a tall German there. I covered my little girl's head with my hands and started to apologize, but he wouldn't listen to what I was saying, and he raised his leather whip high over our heads. I don't know how Chanale managed to free her head from my hands, but she looked straight at him without crying. Maybe it was the look in her eyes that made him lower his hand without hurting us, and he shouted at us instead. I ran home quickly, and only there did I start to cry. Naturally, after this, I seldom went out with Chanale, but she remembered that incident very well. In the ghetto she often said, "How good it is to be here! We don't have to go outside to see Bobeh and Zaideh."

In the second month that we were in the ghetto, on the second day of Rosh Hashanah, we had almost finished praying in the little house where a synagogue had been improvised when ten or more German soldiers and their dogs burst into the ghetto. They summoned Rosenzweig and went straight to the synagogue with him, where they ordered all the Jews to gather in the lot where Maliniak's factory stood. The Germans and their dogs caught all the Jews they could and forced them into the lot.

I was there with Chanale and my nephew Shieleh, as were Henia and her husband. I managed to push a hole out through the fence facing the mountains, and I told the children to run quickly and find Avrumeh, who at that time was working for the Germans as an electrician in a school. The school was not far away, but it was on the other side of the ghetto.

When as many Jews as the Germans could find had gathered on Maliniak's lot, they began to organize us into groups. Members of the Judenrat told us that we were being sent to work, maybe far into Soviet territory. My father and mother were not with us. I didn't know if they had been shot or had escaped. I didn't know what would happen to us. Maybe it was true that we were only going to be sent to work. One thing, though, I was sure of — I would never see my child again. I felt choked with pain. People started to cry quietly and to move about, thinking that maybe one group was better than another. But I had no eyes for what was going on. All I saw was my little Chanale in her red knitted dress running to find her father. The Germans kept us there a few hours, counting and selecting people, and then they yelled to everyone, "Nach Hause gehen!" (Go Home!)

My worried parents met us at the door. They didn't know what had happened. I learned that a German soldier had already seen my father and told him he was too old to work. Yet, my father was over six feet tall and was very handsome, and at sixty-four, he looked younger than he was, having worked very hard all his life. A few minutes later, Avrumeh arrived with Chanale and Shieleh. The children could have been killed amid all the shooting around the ghetto, but they had managed to find Avrumeh and had told him what was going on. Neither we nor Mr. Rosenzweig knew why all the Jews had been gathered in one place. Was it a trial run? Or had there really been an order for workers that was then cancelled? The event gave me a lot to think about — about how to react the next time. But could anyone make plans at a time like this? One thing I decided, though — after this, I wouldn't ever let Chanale out of my sight, not even for a second. She could have easily been killed by a stray bullet!

We hadn't yet gotten over the shock of all this when a girl of fifteen or sixteen came into the ghetto and told us that she and her family, who were from Warsaw, had been on a cattle-car train to Treblinka. This was the first time we heard that name, Treblinka. As the train had passed by some houses not far from the camp, a woman outside had yelled, "They're taking you to Treblinka to die. There are special ovens there built to burn you. Jump! Run and hide wherever you can!" When the girl's mother heard the kind woman's words, she urged her daughter to escape, pleading with her to go and try to live among gentiles. The girl, who was slim, slipped through a small opening in the ceiling of the cattle car, jumped from the train and then walked all night until she finally approached a house. She told the people living there that she was a gentile. From the looks on their faces, though, she realized that they were skeptical of her fabrication and, afraid they would turn her in, she'd walked on, hiding during the day and walking only at night. The girl then arrived in Semiatych and came to the Judenrat office, so we were the first ones to know about her. Soon, almost everybody knew. This kind of news always spread very quickly.

But everybody said that they didn't believe her. Maybe instinctively we just couldn't believe that something so horrible could happen. "The world wouldn't allow it," people insisted. I myself was terrified. A few years earlier I had started to read Hitler's book, *Mein Kampf*. I didn't finish it because it was too frightening to read what Hitler said he would do to the Jews. How could the Germans follow this maniac?

When I told people that I had read much of *Mein Kampf* and that Hitler had openly written about destroying all the Jews — and that that was exactly what he was doing — everybody was angry with me. They accused me of creating panic in the ghetto. Panicky people would do foolish things, and one reckless Jew could cause hundreds to be shot. I tried to hold all my fears inside, but I looked at everyone as though tomorrow they would no longer be alive. But when it came to my Chanale, I couldn't bear the thought that she too would die because she was born of Jewish parents. What could I do? With her dark hair and big black eyes, she looked stereotypically Jewish, so I couldn't even ask any non-Jewish people to take her.

Even though people didn't talk very openly about the news the Warsaw girl had brought — and many tried to dismiss it as only happening in Warsaw, where perhaps there was overcrowding, and sickness, and not enough food — some began to fear that it could happen here, too, and that we might actually be sent to our deaths. Our family started to build a double wall in the attic of our little barn, to hide within. We later found out that other people, having the same idea, had also prepared hiding places in cellars or barns, though these hiding places could only be used for a very short time.

Very early one Sunday morning, at the beginning of October, my aunt Tsippe, who was married to my mother's brother Velvel, and two of her sons, Yankel and Hertzke, as well as Hertzke's wife and their two children, arrived at our house. How had they gotten here? Why had they come? Their whole family lived on a big farm in Wieska-Wieś, a village on the other side of the Bug River. They told us that the month before, they had been dragged out of their homes in Wieska-Wieś and taken to the ghetto in Sterdyń, and that, only a week ago, the Jews had been transported to Treblinka. Worst of all for my mother, they brought the news that her beloved brother Velvel was dead.

Velvel Levin had lived in Wieska-Wieś since birth. He was well respected by his neighbours, and whenever my mother had suggested he sell some merchandise to them because there wasn't a store for miles, he would always answer, "I don't want to be different. I want to live like my neighbours." He lived with his large family, four sons and four daughters, on the farm, and it was his oldest son, Hertzke, who told us the story of what had happened to his father: Having received a tip from a good neighbour that all the Jews from Sterdyń were going to be sent to Treblinka, Hertzke got his father to what he thought was a safe place, working for the Germans, for there had been rumours that Jews in German employ weren't being taken. That was true — Velvel wasn't deported. Instead, he and several others were shot right there where they worked.

We were all shocked, and Mother just couldn't forgive her nephew for arranging that "safe place" for her brother. It didn't help for any of us to explain to her that they had honestly believed that he would be more secure there. "I know only one thing," Mother repeated over and over again. "My brother Velvel isn't alive anymore; he was shot by a German in cold blood."

The thought that a German had shot my mother's brother just like that, for no reason, was hard to imagine. She had always told us about the Germans in Wieska-Wieś, where she too was born and raised. She used to play with German children, who spent the winters there on the Bug River with their families. Mother thought so highly of them. She could never tell us enough about their good behaviour, about their smarts, their culture and so on. And here her own nephew had come to tell her that his father, her brother, had been shot by a German. She felt such grief, and she didn't realize the same fate was likely awaiting us.

During the deportation from the Sterdyń ghetto, my aunt Tsippe, along with her daughter-in-law and her two children — a five-year-old boy and an eighteen-month-old baby — managed to hide in an attic for three days. On the third night, they walked to a farm where they knew the owner wouldn't give them away. Hertzke and his younger brother Yankel, a boy of eighteen, hid in a little wooden pigsty and covered themselves with the dirt from the pigs. There really was no place to hide. The people in the area had been strictly forbidden to let in strangers, and the names of all family members in each home were written on the doors so that someone who didn't belong could be easily identified. "With a child," Hertzke told us, "it is no use even trying. So many parents and children have been caught and shot right on the spot. With a child you can't even hide in a cow pen or a pigsty; the child would cry. And with a child you can't go without regular food, and winter is coming, so it will be too cold to hide outside."

I felt that all this talk was meant for me. I listened without interrupting. But when Avrumeh said, "I won't even try to run away. We have Chanale, and I don't have anybody to turn to," I jumped up and shouted, "Oh, no! I will run with Chanale. I will not wait for them to take us. Let them shoot me in the back while I am running. It is less painful that way."

Crowding in a bit, we made room for our relatives. Aunt Tsippe slept with my mother, Hertzke and Yankel squeezed in with us, and Hertzke's wife and their two children moved in with my brother Shieh, who was living in another part of the ghetto, where Belkes' factory was. Shieh also had two other families living with him: Rikel Lev and her two teenage daughters and a family named Fishelson, who were refugees from Warsaw. Mr. Fishelson was a well-educated man who had worked as a bookkeeper before the Germans occupied

Semiatych and now worked as a secretary in the Judenrat. He had a pass to go outside the ghetto.

A week or so after our relatives arrived, Shieh got permission from the authorities to build a small shack in our garden for my aunt and cousins. My cousins did most of the building, with just a little help, and added a double wall near the door — just in case. We felt it in the air: our end was nearing.

The Will to Live

I often wonder now how I could even have thought of running away. Where did I get my faith in the future? But my mind was always busy. The question of where I would hide didn't stop hammering in my head. *How will we hide? What will I do?* And every time I thought about it, I reached the same decision: I'll try; I have nothing to lose. And I did have some hope. I knew so many gentiles. Maybe one of them would help us.

I was born and raised in Grodzisk, a village with a mixed population of Poles and Russians. Grodzisk had two churches, one Russian and one Polish, a police station, a post office, and a city hall. After World War I, there were several Jewish families there, but most of them eventually moved to other cities or immigrated to North America. My parents had moved to Warsaw in 1936 after facing increasing antisemitism and were among the last Jews to leave Grodzisk, although some did remain in Grodzisk during the war.

When Avrumeh and I had announced that we, too, were leaving, many of them begged us to stay. "Nothing will happen to you," they promised. Of course, we couldn't really trust their promises. After all, what did fine words mean when some of my father's best friends were picketing our store, keeping customers away and sending them off to Polish-owned stores? Some of these people used to come by in the evening and apologize. "We have to do this," they would say. "As good Poles, we have no choice."

I knew that my father was very well-known in Grodzisk, and his name was respected. Every week, on Tuesdays, there was a village market, and people from all the surrounding towns and villages would come either with merchandise to sell or to buy what they needed. Having a store had brought my father into contact with all sorts of people, and he always managed to keep them satisfied.

All around Grodzisk people used to talk about my father's honesty. Once, my father found a purse with a lot of money in it. The man who lost it was running around like a madman. My father asked him, "What happened? Have you perhaps lost some money?" How surprised the man was when my father handed him his purse with all the money inside! He wanted to give my father a reward, but my father refused to accept anything.

Many similar stories were told about my father, and I knew that he had many friends, but which of them would help us? And although I knew their names and what they looked like, I didn't know where they lived, nor could I ask, as that would have been dangerous. There were, however, a few people I had in mind.

For several years, my brother Shieh had owned a dairy in Grodzisk and I had been his bookkeeper, which put me in touch with many people, including a few to whom my brother had lent money. And there was a very poor man named Kilisinski who used to bring milk from his village to the dairy. Shieh always paid him more than he expected, and every day we gave him a big can of buttermilk for his pigs and butter and sweet cream for his children. Every day we would hear him say, "How will I ever repay you?" So, at that critical moment, I kept thinking about Kilisinski, that he would be glad to help us. Only how could we get to him? I knew what village he lived in, but I didn't know in which house.

More than I was counting on Kilisinski — most of all, in fact — I was counting on Vera and Mikolai. Vera and I had gone to school together and had been good friends since childhood. Mikolai, her husband, came from Ciechanowiec but worked in Grodzisk as an assistant secretary. He was much older than his wife and was a good friend of my parents. Not a day passed that he didn't stop by our store, which was just across the street from his office, and not once but several times — for cigarettes, or a cup of tea, or just to rest up or chat. He was always glad to find someone who would listen to him recount his experiences in World War I, and in our house there was always a ready ear. Also, Mother liked to discuss literature and politics with him. I trusted their family more than I did anyone else. Before going into the ghetto, it was to them that we gave our best clothes and linens for safekeeping, in case we would ever have to sell them for food or shelter. When Vera took our things, she cried and said, "If I can ever help you, I will!"

Vera and Mikolai lived just over a kilometre from Grodzisk. As their house stood alone in the woods, it would be easy to reach at night without being seen. I only hoped that we would be able to get out of the ghetto in time. Their house would be our contact place. And since everyone in our family knew where we had hidden our belongings, any one of us who remained alive could go there and ask for them.

On the last Saturday in October, Avrumeh's father, who was living with his family in another part of the ghetto, came to visit. I started in again on what was by now our major topic of conversation.

"What are you thinking of doing if what has happened in other places should also happen here?" I asked.

"Nothing," he said.

"Why?" I persisted.

After all, he was working in his own home outside the ghetto, making suits for the Germans and their wives. He would have a chance, I felt, to ask the gentile woman living in his house for help. I suggested that maybe if he promised to let her keep the house after the war, she would find a way to hide him. But he worried about leaving his wife, who wasn't well, and his married daughter, who had a three-year-old daughter.

"What about your two boys?" I said. "They can live in the woods if they have to. All they need is to find a hiding place for the first few days." I offered them the place behind the double wall in our attic.

"I won't leave my family, and there's no use hiding," he responded.

I became agitated. "If we cling to each other," I insisted, "nobody will survive. If a house is burning, you can't wait to save everything; you just try to save as much as you can."

He left very sad. It was the last time I saw him.

~

Sunday morning, the first of November, seemed to start off well. My aunt and cousins who had arrived the month before from Sterdyń moved into the shed, their new house. And my father returned from his work outside the ghetto with happy news: the Germans and the Soviets were still fighting fiercely at Stalingrad. He thought that the Germans would soon be pushed back by the Soviets. "Now we have hope," he said.

Around noon, Mrs. Rosenzweig called me outside. She said that she had something to tell me but that I had to swear that I would not tell anyone, no one at all, not even my husband, my parents, my brother or my cousins. "What good would the information do me then?" I asked her. "Maybe it will make a difference," she said. She continued to insist that I could not tell anyone and that she was afraid because her husband's life was in danger. Having no choice, I swore silence on the life of my Chanale.

Mrs. Rosenzweig told me that a German official had informed her husband that the next day, November 2, all the Jews from Bielsk Podlaski would be sent away "to work" and warned him that if he let word of this out to anybody, his head would be the first to be chopped off. Bielsk Podlaski was a town about fifty kilometres from our home and, like our own town, was in the county of Bielsk. I realized what this meant: we were going to be deported. I almost fainted. When Mrs. Rosenzweig saw my reaction, she started to cry frantically, saying that she shouldn't have told me, as I would surely make trouble, and her husband would be the first to die.

I thought of my uncle Velvel. Maybe the Germans meant to kill us, or maybe they really did mean to send us to work. Should we go? Should we run? We didn't know what was best, what was safe.

I asked Mrs. Rosenzweig what she thought of hiding in our double wall, but she said that if the Germans found us there, they would shoot us for sure. "But if we're sent to work," she said, "we have hope. We are still young."

I thought to myself, *But Chanale can't work; she's only four.*

We talked for a while, then wiped our tears and went into the house, where Mrs. Rosenzweig watched my every move. My head was throbbing. What should I do? My father was happy with the good news he had heard earlier that morning, but Mother was still crying about her brother Velvel. "Stop crying about your brother," I told her. "Maybe tomorrow we'll all be dead."

Mrs. Rosenzweig looked at me sharply and called me outside again. She pleaded with me, "Don't say anything. It won't help anyway. There's nothing anyone can do. My husband and all the rest of us could be killed for spreading the story." I begged her to let me go over to my brother Shieh in the other part of the ghetto to see if they had heard anything there. After all, Mr. Fishelson, who lived with my brother, was the secretary of the Judenrat.

When I got there, I found that everything was as usual. Shieh was a little surprised to see me. I told him that the previous night I'd had a very bad dream that we were dragged away and pushed into wagons. Someone in the house, I can't remember who, said, "You are always thinking about it, that's why you dream about it. Don't think about it."

"How can you not think about it?" I responded. "Friday somebody told us that the Jews from Brest-Litovsk were all dead. How far are we from there?"

At this point, Shieh turned to Mr. Fishelson and said, "Please, find some excuse and go to the Judenrat office and try to talk to the Germans there. Perhaps you will find something out. Ask the Jewish police to look around, especially on the main roads, to see if more German soldiers are coming into the town."

Mr. Fishelson left. I started to talk to my sister-in-law, Chana, wondering what she was thinking of doing if she found out that something was going to happen the next day. Her answer was the same as my father-in-law's — nothing, and she would not move anywhere. With the influx of refugees there were now more than five thousand Jews in Semiatych. What could happen to them? She wanted to be with everyone else.

I said, "To live together is good, but to die together is not necessary." Chana looked at me but didn't say a word. I tried again. "If you want, come to our section of the ghetto. If we see something happening, we'll hide in our double wall."

"I'm not moving out of my house," she answered. "Whatever happens to everyone will happen to us."

"But you have two daughters. They are so young."

"It's not worth living in a world like this. Better to get it over with."

"Don't be mad at me," I said, seeing that she was angry at my pestering her. "I just can't help myself. I can't sit still, seeing what's happening all around us. We can expect the same here too, any day, maybe even tomorrow. Mr. Rosenzweig said that the Germans have been too good the last few days, and that's not a good sign."

I saw she didn't want to hear anymore, so I turned to Rikel Lev, who also lived in the house, and asked her if she had any plans. After all, her father, Yelke Lev, was a big businessman in Semiatych and knew so many people in the town and in the villages nearby. But she also said, "No, I have no plans, and I'm not trying anything."

Then I said, "Maybe I'm crazy, because I see mothers of teenage children accepting such a destiny, and I, with a child who just turned four twelve days ago, can't stop thinking of what to do and how to escape."

"Maybe you have somebody who will hide you," she said.

"Just like you do. Nobody has prepared a room or a bed for me. As far as I'm concerned, a pigsty to sneak into will be enough. Farmers don't lock their stables or barns, and I hope I'll find someone who will give us a piece of bread. A person can live many months on bread and water."

Rikel responded, "And you really think you can go through all this with Chanale?"

"I don't know if I'll get through it, but one thing I do know, I don't want to be burned in Treblinka. It's easier to be shot!"

I saw I had no support here either. In the meantime, Mr. Fishelson returned from his errand outside the ghetto. He said he hadn't seen anything unusual, though he had seen some Germans and other young men, Ukrainians, coming into town on motorcycles.

"That's it!" I said. "What better proof do we need?"

But somebody in the house retorted accusingly, "She always likes to see things as worse than they are. It's bad enough as it is."

I just said, "I hope to see you again," and I left their house thinking of what Mr. Fishelson had just told us — Germans and other young men coming into town on motorcycles. Wasn't that exactly what my cousin Hertzke told us had happened in Sterdyń, that the day before the roundup, German reinforcements and young men in civilian clothes had come into the town to do the job?

Walking home I met Judith Goldberg and her husband; they were both so young, in their early twenties. Judith asked if there was any news and said I looked very pale. I told her what Mr. Fishelson had said. "One thing I know," I added, "the rope around our necks is being tightened."

But when I asked her whether she would hide among gentiles, especially since she was young, blond and spoke good Polish, her response was, "What about my mother and father?"

"Even if they can't be saved, they don't want you to die, too," I said. "Ask them. We don't have to hold hands. Let everybody find something to hold onto for themselves. Remember, you're blond and young, and that's a good passport to life." Then I said, "If we meet again, don't be angry that I scared you."

When I came home, I told everyone what I had heard at Shieh's. We took a few blankets and some dry bread up to our double wall.

In the evening, my aunt Tsippe's son Shimon arrived from Ciechanowiec. He told us that he had left his sister Chinke and her two children there. Shimon had managed to get out of the ghetto because he was blond and thus looked more "Aryan," and he hoped that we would help him bring Chinke and the children out. He told us that on the same day the Jews had been taken from Sterdyń, they had also been evacuated from Sokołów Podlaski, where Chinke and her family lived. Chinke had escaped with her children and husband, Mayer Greenberg. They hid in the forest where, a week earlier, Mayer had searched out a place and, with Shimon's help, had dug out a large pit there for the family. Because winter was approaching, they wanted to make a sort of bunker for shelter. But one day Shimon had left to look for food, and Chinke and the children were somewhere in the bushes. Shimon came back to the bunker to find Mayer lying dead. He had been shot, his watch and a few other possessions stolen. They buried him right there in the forest, and at night they started to trek to Ciechanowiec, where they had heard there were still Jews in the ghetto.

In Ciechanowiec, they learned that Shimon's brothers and mother were with us, which is what brought him here. When Shimon told us about Mayer, everybody in the house began to cry, even Chanale, who had also known him.

Chanale couldn't understand why Mayer had been shot. What had he done wrong? And she didn't understand what death meant, either. I had always tried to keep Chanale from seeing horrible things. But once, when we were still living across from the Broom, I was sitting with her at the window and we saw a German soldier trying to take Ite-Leya, a mentally challenged girl. Since the German occupation, her parents had kept her at home, but she must have run outside. The German followed her and shot her. I saw it, and so must have Chanale, because now she asked whether Mayer had been shot by the same German as Ite-Leya, and why. As we were crying, I heard Mother say, "I see now that Velvel is better off. He didn't have to see what would happen to his family."

We weren't allowed to have lights on in the ghetto after 7:00 p.m., but that night we just dimmed the light and covered the windows. We didn't talk much. Everyone was nervous. When someone suggested we go to sleep, I advised that it would be better to stay up in case we found out why more Germans had come to town. I also thought that we shouldn't undress for sleep that night. Everyone agreed. Around 11:00 p.m. everyone was tired and wanted to sleep, but I begged them not to, trying to get them to play cards to keep us awake. The men, including my cousin Hertzke, started up a game. I put Chanale to sleep, but I took off only her dress and put it next to the bed along with her winter coat and white angora hat. Mother lay down in her clothes. Father watched the men playing cards.

At one in the morning, Mr. Rosenzweig, who had permission to go out at night, said he would go to the gate to see if everything was as usual. Ten minutes after he'd left, a Jewish boy from the ghetto police ran into the house and said, gasping, "The German commandant wants Rosenzweig in his office at once!" Mrs. Rosenzweig told him that her husband was at the gate and he should look for him there.

We woke up Mother, and Hertzke ran to get his mother, wife and children, who that very day had moved into the new little shed in the garden, and his brothers, Yankel and Shimon, who hadn't even had time to rest after coming from Ciechanowiec. I dressed Chanale in her coat, hat and shawl, led her to the door and instructed her not to move until I got back. I put a second dress on top of the one I was wearing, and on top of that, my coat and a woollen shawl. My father climbed up to the attic to get a coat for Aunt Tsippe. In the dark, it was taking him a while to find it.

As we were getting ready, Mr. Rosenzweig rushed in, sweating, and notified us, "The commandant ordered me to call together every-one in the Judenrat and the Jewish police right now. When I asked him, 'Why now? Isn't it at six o'clock that you wake the Jews for work?' he screamed at me, 'I order you, right now!' I said, 'Okay, I'll call them now,' and was glad he let me go." As Mr. Rosenzweig left the house, he turned back at the door to say, "I'm running, and I think you all should, too. This is it!"

Avrumeh ran to the door after him, took Chanale's hand and dis-appeared into the night. I called to my father, who was still looking for a coat for Aunt Tsippe. "Father, we're going! Hurry down at once!" But he couldn't let Tsippe leave without a coat. Mother was wearing a black winter coat, and her face was white as a sheet. I turned to go. I could see Chanale's white hat in the darkness and I caught up with her and Avrumeh in the yard and took her free hand. "Whatever happens," I whispered to her, "you have to be absolutely silent. No matter what."

Nowhere to Go

As we crossed through the barbed-wire fence, we saw other people running as well. We wanted to go to the mountains, but just as we were about to head there, we heard shooting from that direction. Mr. Rosenzweig was leading us, with my brother-in-law Sruleh following right after him. They turned in the direction of the forest. I lifted Chanale onto my back and told Avrumeh to follow Rosenzweig. When he was two steps ahead of us, a bullet fell right between us. Chanale tried to jump. I held her even tighter and warned her to be quiet. But in my heart, I was sure we would never make it, and I hoped that if we had to die, the same bullet would strike both of us together.

Then somebody tried to pass me in the dark and touched my elbow. Turning, I recognized my nephew Shieleh. I told him that his father was in front of us. But where was his mother? He said his mother was still waiting for his grandfather, who had not yet come down from the attic. I also saw my cousin Yankel carrying his nephew, a child of two and a half, whose parents had been seized on the streets of Warsaw. "Ruchl, take the baby, too," he said to me in a whisper. "Do you think I can carry two children on my back?" I answered. He left without responding.

I was soaking wet with sweat. I was wearing two woollen dresses, a sweater and a coat, and I was still carrying Chanale on my back. At first, I kept running, but when I couldn't anymore, I just begged

Avrumeh to run on after Rosenzweig while I put Chanale down and walked with her and Shieleh. I had forgotten to put on Chanale's leggings, and she kept complaining that her legs were cold. Chanale didn't understand what was happening, but young Shieleh, who knew what it was all about, was trembling with both cold and fear.

As Rosenzweig and Avrumeh reached the forest, the new day started to dawn. I saw them stop near a tree and wait for us. My brother-in-law Sruleh was not too far behind them; perhaps he couldn't run as quickly as them or maybe he had been thinking, "Where am I running without my wife and only son?" He had also left his mother, Gitke Zoltak, and two brothers and their families behind in the ghetto. As we came closer, he saw his son and waited for us. Together we went deeper into the forest. Chanale was ice cold. I took off one of my dresses and put her feet into the sleeves, tying the waist with a belt to make leggings.

The sun began to rise. All around it was quiet. The only sound we heard was the birds singing. There was not a sign here of what we had left behind in Semiatych. Then, as we ran further, we heard rounds and rounds of shooting. Everybody started thinking about their families. Rosenzweig's wife had been near him when he announced the news of the roundup, as had his two children, Chazkel and Ruzka. Where were they now? What had happened?

I knew where my father had been when we left. Maybe he still hoped that he wouldn't have to run, but I had seen him put Mother's heart pills in his pocket, and all evening he had whispered, "Mother should only be well." His Rivche-leibn! My mother's name was Rivka, but he always called her Rivche-leibn — Rivka, my life. Where were they now? And my sister Henia, who had been waiting for Father to come down from the attic, even though her only son had just run out the door? And my brother Shieh and his family? Did he have time to escape? And did his wife, Chana, and his children follow him? Chana hadn't wanted to struggle for a life like this.... And my husband's family, who knew what was happening to them? I knew that the two young boys, Yudel and Srulek, would have found it easier to run. But did they do it?

As we thought about the people we had left behind, the sun rose. It was time for breakfast, or it would have been under different circumstances. As the hours went by, we grew hungry, and we realized that we didn't even have a crust of bread for Chanale. I had prepared all kinds of bundles to take along, but in all the panic I had forgotten to take those. All I had now was a little bag of sugar and candy, and some apples that I had put in my pocket.

Around two o'clock in the afternoon we spotted from afar a man walking through the woods. Unlike the rest of us, he wasn't carrying anything. Rosenzweig decided he would talk to him. The man, a Pole, told Rosenzweig that the Germans had placed automatic guns on the mountains facing the ghetto and all around the ghetto, as well. Jews who ran away were shot, and now all the bodies were being thrown into one big grave.

Rosenzweig offered the man money and asked him if there was a possibility of hiding somewhere. "Not right now. I have to see what's going on," the man said, and then added, "Our people are no good. They were waiting for this." We knew what he meant. After the Jews were all killed, the Poles would have their homes, furniture and everything the Germans did not take for themselves. Rosenzweig pointed to Chanale and begged him to bring bread for the young children. The man left and came back with a piece of bread, but only enough for one meal for the two children. We understood our position, that a piece of bread was too much to ask for.

We started to plan what we would do next. I asked Rosenzweig if he had plans for himself. He wasn't obligated to us, and as a man alone and with some money, he had better chances by himself. I told him what I had in mind. We had to get to the vicinity of Grodzisk. From the far side of Semiatych, where we were at the time, the distance would take us two nights to walk, and on the way we would have to cross two major roads. It was risky, I knew. But as I explained over and over, even if we couldn't be sure of the outcome, our only hope was to find someone who would help us.

Night was approaching. I put Chanale to sleep on my lap and we kept planning. I saw that Rosenzweig had no confidence in my plans and realized that he didn't want to go with us. There were too many of us, and the children were also a problem. I started to persuade Avrumeh to go with Rosenzweig. We'd separate. I explained that a man alone had a better chance of finding a hiding place than if he were with a group. Before the war, Avrumeh had worked as an electrician in a grain mill for a very nice Pole named Lupko, who had liked him and his work. I begged him to go there, certain he could hide among the sacks of grain in the daytime and work at night in exchange for food. I tried to convince Avrumeh, just as I had insisted earlier, that we all had to look out for ourselves — otherwise no one would survive. I believed that there was no reason for all of us to die together, when one of us might survive alone.

Of one thing I was absolutely certain: Lupko wouldn't harm anyone. Rosenzweig, who liked the idea, helped me persuade Avrumeh. He and Avrumeh would go to Lupko's; Sruleh and I and the children would go to Grodzisk, where Mikolai lived. We agreed that Mikolai's was the place where we would leave messages for each other. Though it wasn't easy to persuade him, Avrumeh finally left with Rosenzweig. The rest of us would stay where we were until the next day, when, in the evening, we would set out for the Grodzisk area.

It didn't take half an hour before we heard two shots. I said to Sruleh, "That's Avrumeh and Rosenzweig — gone. What have I done? Why did I tell them to go off by themselves? How can I live with myself, knowing that I sent Avrumeh out to meet those bullets?"

Sruleh tried to reassure me that I had the best of intentions, that I had sent them out there meaning only the best for them. He admired my courage in wanting to save my husband even though that meant remaining behind, alone with Chanale.

Sruleh and I passed the night whispering about this and similar topics. The two children slept soundly. Then, at daybreak, we heard some noises, followed by the sound of whispering — and then from behind a bush came Avrumeh and Rosenzweig! It turned out that they had also heard the two shots, realized that they had been fired on by the men guarding the tracks from Nurzec to Semiatych, and so decided to come back. But they couldn't find us. It took them a whole night to locate us. Needless to say, we were overjoyed to see one another. Once again, we started to plan what we would do.

We didn't see a soul all the next day. We thought that perhaps we would see some Jews who had escaped, but we didn't.

The sun was shining through the trees and bushes as though nothing at all had happened. Chanale was ready to play. She just couldn't understand why we had all run away from home, though she did remember that on our last evening there we were all crying because Mayer had been shot. Over and over, she asked, "Why did we have to run if the Germans shot Mayer?"

I gave the children a bit of sugar and candy and I started to teach Chanale what the word "dead" meant, what being shot meant. But it was very hard to explain to a child of four why the Germans wanted to shoot us. And where were her Bobeh and Zaideh? Why weren't they with us? And Henia? She loved them all very much. One thing I repeated to her hundreds of times: No matter what, she couldn't talk loudly; if she wanted to sneeze, she should hold her nose with two fingers. And she must not cry at all.

Rosenzweig was pacing from one bush to another. When it started to get darker, I said to him, "Well, what are your plans now? Are you going alone? If so, good luck. But if you're willing to come with us, we'll be glad to have you." He decided to go alone. We agreed that he had a better chance that way and wished him luck. We kissed him goodbye and he left.

∽

When we had to leave the forest, I was terribly frightened, but we had no choice. We had no food at all, and it was freezing at night. I have a very poor sense of direction, but Avrumeh had been in the area once, so I explained to him where Grodzisk was and that we'd have to cut across two major roads, the road from Nurzec to Semiatych and the very busy road from Bielsk Podlaski. We decided that we would cross only the road from Nurzec that night and would then try to sleep a little, since we hadn't slept for two nights.

We started to walk across the fields, afraid to use even the smallest roads in case we met someone — such criminals were we, escaping our death sentence. The fields were frozen, and after walking for a few hours, we didn't know where we were. Since I was the only one who spoke Polish without a Yiddish accent, Avrumeh and Sruleh insisted I go into a house and ask. But I was scared and didn't want to, so we found a few bushes where we could rest. We all fell asleep.

When we woke up, we couldn't remember which direction we had come from and which direction we had to go in. After arguing for some time I gave in, knowing that my sense of direction couldn't be trusted. The road we had to cross turned out to be a very short distance from the place where we had slept. By the time we crossed to the other side, there was too much light for us to continue, and we had to find some woods to hide in for the day. Soon we saw a grove of trees. Although we were not far from a village, it was too late in the day for us to be choosy, so we walked deeper into the grove.

After an hour or so, we spotted a young man walking straight toward us. We were frightened, but when he came closer, my brother-in-law Sruleh recognized him as one of the customers who used to come into his clothing store before the war. There was something odd in the young man's voice. I sensed that he was disappointed about something, but I didn't know what. He told us matter-of-factly that the Jews in Semiatych were still in the ghetto and that those who had tried to escape had been shot to death. Before he walked off, he made a point of telling us that many were already dead.

About half an hour later, maybe less, another man was walking briskly toward us. It was Theodore, whom Sruleh considered a very good friend — and so he turned out to be. Theodore had come to tell us that our recent visitor had intended to steal our clothing and probably hadn't carried out his scheme only because there were too many of us. The man was scouring the woods for Jews to rob, Theodore informed us, and had actually told Theodore about us. Theodore was afraid that he had gone to bring help and suggested a spot where we could hide for the day. He also brought bread for us. But the most exciting thing he told us was that my sister Henia had been at his house the night before. She had come running, wearing only a dress. He gave her a jacket, and she went on to the home of Babinska, a woman whom my brother Shieh had once saved from being sent to Siberia by the Soviets. Shieh had hidden Babinska, the daughter of a rich landowner and the wife of a Polish captain, in a locked room for a few weeks and then, after preparing documents for her, had transported her to the other side of the Bug River, where she would be safe. Babinska was now living with her sister and her sister's family three kilometres from Grodzisk in a house in a forest.

Theodore also told us that after my sister left, my mother showed up at his house. Mother hadn't known where he lived but somehow arrived there. She too had continued on to Babinska's house. When we asked him if Mother had told him anything about Father, he said no. Before he left, he told us where to wait and promised to come back before dark with something for us to eat. After sunset, he returned with bread and a bottle of warm milk for the children.

When we finished eating, we started to walk toward Grodzisk in better spirits because we had heard that my mother and sister had managed to escape and because we now had proof that there were still some people who were willing to help us. After a few hours of night walking, we were again lost. This time, though, having experienced such kindness from Theodore, I decided to go into a house and ask what the name of the village was.

Inside, the man of the house was sleeping, and the woman asked me where I'd come from. I told her and also admitted that I was a Jew who had escaped from the Germans. "Don't tell anyone you're Jewish!" she warned. "You have a perfect Polish accent. Go very far away from here where nobody knows you, and you'll find work."

When I told her I had a four-year-old child and my husband outside she said, "I wish you luck, but it will be very hard."

We were on the right road but still had far to go to reach Mikolai's house before daybreak. It was almost five kilometres to Grodzisk, and then we would have to find the narrow road leading to Mikolai's house. As we walked, I was not quite sure that the road we were on was the right one. Having trekked all night, we were all very tired, especially Shieleh, who was walking as well. I suggested that Avrumeh and the children rest for a few minutes while Sruleh and I walk on a bit further to find out if we were on the right road. Everybody agreed. Walking along with Sruleh, I realized that the road we were looking for was much further off.

A dense fog was spreading over everything, and we couldn't even see from one bush to another. We decided to go back to Avrumeh and the children. But how alarmed we were when we couldn't find them! I became hysterical, blaming myself and running from bush to bush like a madwoman. Sruleh couldn't keep up with me and he was pleading with me to calm down, but I kept running and crying, "What have I done, bringing you all here, right under the noses of the Germans to be shot right where I was born?"

Eventually, I saw two houses: one large, solid, belonging to people who were well-off; the other, across the road from it, small and obviously poorer. Now we would have to knock and ask where we were. But on which door? Like every other decision we made in these months, our choice here could be fatal. Better at the poor house, Sruleh soon suggested. We walked over, and I turned the doorknob. The door opened. As we stepped in, I saw a woman in the room and four male heads peeking out from under blankets to check who had come in. I completely froze on seeing those four heads. *This is the end*, I thought to myself. But the woman recognized me and called out sympathetically, "Oh, who do I see here? Ephraim's daughter!" Relieved, unbelievably relieved by the pity in her voice, I asked her where we were. "In Aleksandrowo," she replied, "and surely you knew my husband." Did I ever! She was the wife of Edward, who was the head of the picketers who had marched in front of my parents' store. He had been in jail on and off, though not for picketing, and she told me that he was no longer alive. She asked me not to think badly of her husband, saying that he had only picketed my father's store because it was what was expected of "good" Poles.

Nevertheless, it felt as though all my blood was thickening from terror. But I was already there, and there was nothing for me to do but tell her the whole story, that I had been with my husband and two children and that I had lost them in the bushes. I had forty zloty on me, two twenty-zloty pieces. "Here, I have forty zloty — take twenty and tell me where I can find them. I want to die together with my child," I said to her and continued to appeal to her as a mother and in the good name of my father.

As I begged and pleaded, she turned to the four men — three were her sons, one was her brother — and said to one of her sons, "Wladek, get dressed and take them back to her family." I grabbed her hands and kissed them. I described to Wladek where I had turned to the right near the grain mill, told him approximately how long we had walked, and that Avrumeh and Chanale had sat down under a big tree. Well, he took us straight there, and we found everyone sleeping. When they woke up and we started on our way again, we let Wladek accompany us only a short way because we didn't want him to know where we were going. I gave him the twenty zloty, and although he did not actually want to take half of the last money we had, he felt he had to since I had already mentioned it to his mother. We thanked him, and Avrumeh asked him whether he would be willing to hide us in their barn for a day or so if we needed a place. Wladek explained to us that the large house across from theirs was his uncle's, who was the *soltys*, the head of the village council, and that the man we had seen in his house was another uncle who had come to visit from another village. "We're afraid of them," he said, "but if you have to, you can spend a night or two in our barn."

It was already light when we reached Mikolai's house. When we tried the door to the little shed where they kept the firewood, it was open, so we all went in and waited for the family to wake up. Finally, we saw Vera coming, carrying food for the pigs. When I walked out to meet her, she almost dropped the pail with the food. I told her who was with me and asked if I could stay in a corner of her big barn for a while. She was so stunned that she couldn't say anything except, "Oh my God!" and then she ran into the house.

We waited. What else could we do? Mikolai came and said how sorry he was about everything that had happened to us. Since I'd fallen into water several times when I was running to find Avrumeh and the children, my feet were wet and I was shivering. He noticed this and told me he would bring us something warm, returning after a few minutes with a pot of oatmeal.

We hadn't quite finished eating when the door opened and my sister Henia walked in! She looked so relieved at seeing her husband and son alive. It turned out that she had spent only a few hours at Babinska's, whose life our brother had once saved. We had all counted on her, but the night that Henia and Mother took shelter in the straw in her barn, she told them that they could not stay. Henia left, figuring that if she went away, Babinska might hide just Mother. Henia hoped that if anyone in the family had survived, Mikolai would know about it.

While I was still eating, Henia said to me, "Father has been shot dead." My food stuck in my throat. So did my words. Not a single tear came to my eyes; they stayed inside.

Henia told me that Mother and Father had left the house a few minutes after we did. By then the Germans and their helpers had caught up with the people who were running for the barbed-wire fence, and a bullet had hit Mother's arm when she was running with Father. A girl who had been caught at the fence was screaming terribly, and it was then that Henia lost track of our parents. Her own coat was caught on the barbed wire, and she unbuttoned it and left it there to save herself. That's why she had come to Theodore's wearing no coat.

As we were telling each other everything that had happened to us, Mikolai walked in and informed us that his wife was very scared and that we couldn't stay. All our pleading and begging didn't help. Regardless of the fact that we had nowhere to go and that it was daylight and people would recognize us, Mikolai was against allowing Henia and her husband, Sruleh, and son, Shieleh, to stay for even one second. We assumed he didn't want to have so many people there but we finally managed to convince him to let Henia and her family stay until it got dark. In the evening, they set out for Zalewski's house, on a farm a few kilometres away from Mikolai's, where Henia had left many valuables.

An hour after Henia and her family left, Mikolai ordered us out too. I showed him my feet, which were all blistered and bruised from walking in my wet shoes. I was still shivering with cold, never mind from everything I had just heard. I begged him to let us stay for two days. We'd rest and our bruises would heal. We didn't know where we would go after that. If he, our best friend, wouldn't help us, who would? I asked him if it was only his wife who didn't want us. If she was the problem, we could hide in the straw, where she wouldn't find us, and he would only have to bring us a piece of bread for Chanale. But all my appeals didn't help. He said that his wife was sick and he couldn't take the risk.

I asked him to give me some of the things I'd left there, and he brought me two sheets. I convinced him to let us stay one night, promising we'd leave as soon as it started to get light. "If not," I said, "you can kill us right here; at least that's a way out." That night I really envied all the people who had stayed behind in the ghetto and, most of all, I envied my father, who had gotten it over with once and for all. Had my sister-in-law Chana and Rikel been right, that it wasn't worth living in a world like this? And had my father-in-law been right when he said it was no use trying?

But most of all I couldn't stop thinking: What did my father think when he came down from the attic and found that I hadn't waited? I had run out like a crazy woman after seeing that Chanale had disappeared through the door. Did my father understand? Or was he very disappointed in his daughter, whom he trusted?

I was still trying to think about what to do and where to go when morning dawned, and I couldn't stop thinking about what had happened up till now, my bringing all of them here. And for what?

One thought kept running through my mind: "We'll leave at dawn." I had promised that we would, and we had to save this place for an emergency and stay on good terms, too, since we had so many valuable things here that we would want to come back for some day. So, when it started to get light out, we left the barn, taking along an old coat Mikolai had given us to cover ourselves with when he saw us shivering with cold. Neither Avrumeh nor I had the strength to carry Chanale. I'd had so much hope before. Now it was all gone.

Seeking Shelter

We managed to reach a small forest before the sun rose, and we settled under a bush on the frozen earth. Mikolai had given us matches to make a fire, but we were afraid somebody would see it. At nightfall we started to walk back toward Aleksandrowo. I knew the owner of a grain mill there, Niminski. But we didn't know which house was his and had to take the risk and ask at the mill. Frightened, cold, hungry and very tired, we walked toward the light of the mill.

The door of the mill was open and, having no other choice, we walked straight in. Niminski was there. He recognized me, but he didn't say a word. He stood there staring at us and as tears ran down his cheeks, I knew I could trust him. Before I had a chance to say more than a few words, the door opened again, and who walked in but Wladek, the same young man who had helped me find Avrumeh and the children. Avrumeh went over to Wladek and started to beg him to hide us in his barn for a few days. We promised to give him the two sheets we had taken with us, and a black suit and a coat and many other things that we had hidden away.

Wladek told us that we could come to his barn for a few days. As he started to walk out, Niminski went over to him and said, "Wladek, do help these people. They are innocent; their enemies are our enemies. God will help you for it. I can't keep them; too many people come here." Wladek didn't answer but just walked outside to wait for us.

Then Niminski invited us into his house for something to eat. His wife was also very sympathetic. They gave us a lot of food and explained, again, that they couldn't hide us, for too many people showed up at the grain mill. He felt that Wladek would help us if we had something of value to give him. We knew that Wladek had two brothers, one older and one younger, and their mother also lived with them. But we would have to take a chance with them.

When we met Wladek outside, he had already managed to go home and check with his mother, who also agreed to take us in. I can't say that I was entirely comfortable about what we were doing, as I was afraid it might be a trap. But as I said, we had no other offer. I felt humiliated and ashamed going back there, for it meant that we hadn't been able to find a hiding place with supposedly good friends.

After we exchanged a few words, we were shown to their barn, an old wooden building with the wind blowing right through the walls. There was not very much straw for warmth. But at that point it looked like a palace to us. This was the first night that I didn't have to worry where we would go in the morning. Covering ourselves with our clothes and the scant straw, we had our first real night's sleep since leaving our beds in the ghetto.

In the morning, Wladek brought us breakfast and told us that around noon, one of their neighbours would be coming to the barn to cut some straw on the cutting machine they shared, and that we'd have to be very quiet. We promised, and for what felt like the hundredth time, I warned Chanale how very quiet she had to be.

At noon, the neighbour came to cut his straw, with Wladek following at his heels. They worked for two hours as we lay silently in the straw, petrified to make the slightest move lest he discover us. I'm sure that if they hadn't been talking all the while, they would have heard our hearts hammering in our chests. Luckily, they did talk — and Wladek good and loud, so that his partner wouldn't hear any chance noise we might make.

They talked about Jews, the topic of the day. We learned that there were still Jews in the Semiatych ghetto who were being guarded by Germans and other men in civilian clothes, and that people from the surrounding villages were coming to the town to buy things. Wladek's neighbour informed him that the Germans had promised to sell all the Jews' belongings, and that they were bound to be cheap. After all, he concluded forcefully, "The goods didn't cost the Germans anything." The things we heard!

After the man had gone, Wladek came back and apologized to us for the things he had said about Jews. He didn't really mean them, he said, but his neighbour needed to think he felt the same way he did. "To me all people are the same, and all that matters is that they're good and decent," Wladek told us.

We had to believe him. What choice did we have after Mikolai, our friend, had refused us even a corner of his barn? But, in fact, Wladek was telling the truth. After two days in the barn, it looked like he would let us stay for a while, especially after we gave him the two sheets and the twenty zloty we still had, and after we promised him Avrumeh's new black suit — worn only once, at our wedding.

Now that our shelter was taken care of, at least for the time being, I started to think about Mother. Had Babinska let her stay there after Henia had left? This was our only hope, and we very much wanted to believe in it. After all, where would Mother go all alone with a wounded arm if Babinska put her out?

I couldn't help these thoughts churning around in my mind. But what could I do? After struggling with myself for two days and nights, I told Avrumeh that I had to go and look for Mother, if only Wladek and his mother would promise to keep Chanale and him till I came back. *If* I came back. I knew what this meant to my husband, but he didn't say no. Wladek and his mother also agreed, and I told them that I'd bring back the black suit we had promised, since it was at Mikolai's.

The barn could only be locked and unlocked from the outside, so that evening Wladek was supposed to open the barn and let me out. But somebody stopped in to visit, and he couldn't come. On the second evening there was a snowstorm, and on the third, something else happened, though I can't now remember what.

Finally, on the fourth evening, I waited for Wladek to come and open the barn, torn between the feeling that I had to go to look for my mother and the fear and guilt of leaving my husband and child. What if I didn't come back and we got separated? Avrumeh didn't know anyone here. Immersed in these thoughts I saw through one of the many cracks in the wall that Wladek was approaching. I kissed Avrumeh and Chanale and got ready to set out. Imagine my surprise and joy when Wladek walked into the barn and said, "Your mother is at the house!"

My mind raced. What power had kept me from going? I wouldn't have found her anyway. How had she known where to find us?

Wladek told us we could go into his house. The windows had been covered, and they locked the door behind me when I walked in. There was my mother, sitting near the oven and white as a ghost; she looked as if she'd just stepped out of a grave. We hugged but didn't say a word.

Wladek broke the silence. "How did your mother find you? It means that somebody must know where you are and it's dangerous for you to stay." Mother couldn't answer. Trembling with fear, she held me tighter and cried, "Ruchale, don't let them chase me away!" I answered that now only death would separate us.

Avrumeh slipped off his wedding ring and gave it to Wladek. After begging, crying and promising all kinds of things, we were finally allowed to go back to the barn.

How *did* Mother know where to find us? She told us that after my sister left, Babinska told Mother that she couldn't endanger her own sister and family by keeping her. Babinska said she knew how much she owed my brother for saving her, but she wasn't alone in the house, and she was sure that Mother wouldn't want to have it on her conscience that she was putting everyone in danger. How ironic that Babinska had appealed to Mother's conscience!

That night, Mother left to look for another place. She eventually came to a village called Kosianka and followed the only light she could see to a grain mill owned by a widow named Timinska, whom she knew very well. Timinska bandaged Mother's arm and gave her some good food. For a few days, Mother helped her by washing dishes, peeling potatoes and doing all kinds of sewing, which she could do very well. Just as Mother was beginning to regain her strength, someone caught a glimpse of her through a window and started questioning Timinska. Though Timinska wanted Mother to stay on, Mother knew the danger they were both in, and decided to go where she assumed Henia had gone, to Zalewski's, hoping that he would hide her, too. It was at Zalewski's that my mother learned from Henia that Avrumeh, Chana and I had escaped, and that Henia had left us at Mikolai's.

After only a day, Zalewski told Mother to go. Otherwise, he said, Henia and her family would have to leave, too. Worried that by coming she had spoiled a good shelter for Henia, Mother told her to stay on and that she would go to Mikolai's to look for us. But how terribly disappointed my mother was to learn that Mikolai had turned us out and didn't want her either. Mikolai, who had always admired her, didn't even let her into his house.

Mother told us she had only one desire left at that point — to find us to make sure that we were alive, and then to die. Mikolai pointed out the direction on the nameless road we had taken and, once again, she started to walk at night. By this point she was so worn out from being driven from one place to another that she would have willingly sat down and frozen to death. Luckily, she suddenly saw a light in the distance, and the light drew her on and on until she reached Niminski's grain mill. Niminski hid her in a locked room for two days, fed her well to build up her strength, told her that we were probably at Wladek's and showed her the way. That's how she found us.

Mother slept for two nights and a day. When she had rested, I asked her how Father had died. This is what she told me: Just two minutes after we had left, Father came down from the attic with a coat for Aunt Tsippe, and the three of them all ran out together. They had only gotten to the middle of the garden when the bullet grazed her elbow. Father tightened his grip on her hand under his arm and whispered, "Rivche-leibn, just keep well. We'll live through the Germans, you'll see."

At the barbed-wire fence, they lost Henia, but Tsippe and her daughter-in-law and her two children were now with them. Together they walked some distance away from the ghetto. But at daybreak, they were afraid to walk any further. They saw a group of Jews sitting in a small valley — Maita Lev, Yankel the Blecher (the tinsmith) and his fourteen-year-old daughter and a few others — and they went over and sat down with them. While they were sitting there, Mother saw a boy running and recognized him as Chaim Steinberg, the ten-year-old (and youngest) son of her best friend, Ruchl Steinberg. She called him over, and he lay down among them.

It was damp and cold, and my cousin's baby started to cry. They tried to cover him, to give him something to eat, but he cried on, and before long, they saw two German soldiers coming toward them. Mother, in her perfect German, started to beg. They'd go back to the ghetto, she told one, and they were sorry they had run. Seeing the Germans cock their rifles, she brought her head down to the ground, face down. It was so quiet there. No one let out a peep. There was only the sound of shooting.

She felt a German touch the back of her head to make sure she was dead. Then she heard nothing until she came to, to the screaming of the fourteen-year-old girl who had been shot in the stomach. Everyone else was lying quiet as could be. And among them, Father, his open eyes staring up at her. He had probably still believed that if his Rivche-leibn spoke to the Germans, they'd let them go back to the ghetto. At first Mother thought Father was alive because there was no blood on him. She touched him, kissed him on the forehead, but he didn't move.

She took the heart pills out of his pocket but forgot to take the money he had prepared. Mother started to walk. It was daytime now, and the two yellow patches stood out clearly on the front and back of her black coat. But she didn't know what she was doing. Her feet just moved automatically, and she kept on walking the rest of that day.

Just as it was becoming dark, Mother reached a village. She knocked on the first door she saw. The young woman who answered it turned out to be from Grodzisk. Mother told her what had happened in the ghetto, but the young woman already knew everything. She washed the dry blood from Mother's arm, in return for which Mother took off the golden earrings she was wearing and gave them to the woman's little girl. After giving Mother something warm to eat and realizing that she was in no condition to walk any further, the woman told her to sleep in the barn because she wasn't sure how her husband would react to seeing her. In the morning she brought Mother warm milk and bread, but when she finished eating, she told her she would have to leave. Mother cried bitterly, but the young woman said she couldn't help her, as her husband wanted to kill her for allowing Mother to stay in the first place. So Mother left.

The second door she came to was Theodore's. There she learned that Henia had been at his house and had gone on to Babinska's, which was at least thirty kilometres away. Hearing that Henia was alive gave Mother the courage to follow her. On the way, when she knocked on a door to ask for water, a woman jumped out and tried to snatch the warm shawl right off her head, telling her, "You won't need it, you'll soon die anyway." Mother managed to run away.

I still have that shawl, and I cherish it very much.

~

One morning Wladek told us that a watchman had found a nine-year-old Jewish boy in the Czarny forest and brought him to the Germans in Grodzisk. We begged Wladek to go to Grodzisk and find out what had become of the boy. The next day, Wladek told us that the Germans had thrown the boy into a cellar beneath their office for the night, and the following day, two Germans — afraid that only one wouldn't be able to handle a nine-year-old boy? — took him to a beautiful little forest called Gaj. They told him to run, and then they shot him. A Polish boy buried him. The boy told Wladek that the dead boy was from Brańsk and that his mother had left him in the forest in the hope that if he were alone somebody would take him in, for he could have worked as a shepherd. Hearing this, we were all speechless. Chanale grabbed onto my neck, crying, "You won't leave me in the forest, Mama?"

I said, "Of course not." What else could I answer? She already knew that she belonged to the same type of people as that unfortunate boy. Only she couldn't understand how anyone could tell the difference between her and other children playing freely on the street.

Before that incident I had sometimes thought of maybe trying to find a nice gentile family who would want to take Chanale in and bring her up. If I lived, I would be able to take her back and if not, she would be theirs. But I always came to the conclusion that she would probably be brought up to hate Jews, which of course I didn't want. And then I would remember the story of King Solomon and the two women who each claimed the same child as her own. Judging the case, King Solomon ordered that the child be cut in half and that each woman be given one part. The false mother agreed, but when the other woman screamed, "Give her the child!" Solomon knew who the real mother was. I thought that if I had no other way to save Chanale, I would rather give her away to be taken care of. I could imagine Avrumeh and me dying, but I couldn't possibly think of her having to die. But the story of that boy taught me differently. His poor mother had probably also thought that her child had a greater chance of surviving if he was alone.

Mother was talking, almost to herself. What had happened to the Germans? What had gotten into them? Shooting fourteen people, among them my cousin's baby! She alone had walked out alive. Now she heard that they had shot that little boy. "Who are they fighting?" she asked. "Helpless and innocent children?" It was so hard for her to believe that Germans could do these things. It had never happened in the history of humankind.

A day later, Wladek brought the news that he had seen a young Jewish couple from Semiatych who had jumped from a train heading to Treblinka. They begged him to bring them bread, and he was on his way there now. We asked him to find out their names and whether they knew anything about Shieh Kejles, our brother. A few hours later he came back and told us their names and that they had last seen Shieh in the ghetto. They thought he had probably been taken to the trains. We couldn't believe it — our big brother Shieh, taken without resisting. Shieh, who always had to have his own way. But just as other unbelievable things were happening, maybe this too had happened. I knew what it meant to Mother. One pain heavier than the last was falling on our hearts.

The next morning, we didn't see anybody from Wladek's family and couldn't understand why. Finally, in the late afternoon, Wladek ran into the barn to tell us that they had all gone to Nurzec to buy things that the Jews had left behind and that the Germans were now selling. They had taken a few bottles of homemade whisky with them and on the road had met Germans who looked into the wagon and found the bottles. Wladek told us that they took his address and warned him that they would come the next day to see if he had any more at home. It was clear that we would have to leave. He told us that if we hid somewhere else for two weeks, we could come back when things were quiet, and to bring the black suit.

I couldn't think of anything better to do than to go and look for Kilisinski, whom Shieh used to help out. I had been so disappointed by Mikolai and Vera, and I had little faith that Kilisinski would be much better, but I couldn't think of an alternative. I asked where Kilisinski lived, and we went there. Kilisinski didn't seem very afraid of hiding us. He got right down to business, wanting to know what we had with us and how we would pay him. I named lots of things that I could bring him and told him that I still had my gold watch on my wrist, as did Avrumeh, and that I had two gold pieces sewn into my brassiere. Kilisinski wasn't sure if the watches were of much value but took a gold piece and showed us to the attic. His son, a boy of twelve, tagged along and watched our every move.

The next day Kilisinski took us to his old dilapidated barn, which had very little straw in it, and brought us some barely cooked cabbage. Mother said it looked like the food he gave to the pigs. She was sure he was being intentionally spiteful and didn't trust him. "I wouldn't trust him either," I said, "if I had anywhere else to go."

So we passed another night, hungry and cold. We couldn't fall asleep. At three in the morning, we heard footsteps. Mother heard Kilisinski's heavy breathing and called out his name. He was surprised to see us all awake and asked why. We told him we were very cold. He brought us things to cover ourselves with and told us not to think about anything, just to try and sleep. At five o'clock, he was back, moving very quietly so as not to be heard. Surprised, we asked, "What are you doing here?" His eyes were gleaming, and he was trembling. He didn't answer our question. When he left again, Mother said her heart told her we should leave before something very bad happened. But where to? We stayed on through the day. Every hour, he asked what we had with us and what we could give him. In the evening he announced he was going to a village meeting. Mother again urged us to leave — she was afraid that he was on his way to the Germans to report us. This time we did set out, making sure, of course, that no one in his family saw us go.

Much later we found out the reason for Kilisinski's night visits: he had come carrying an axe, planning to murder us. We learned this from my cousin Luba Licht, who was hidden in a locked room in the house of a neighbour with whom Kilisinski had shared his intentions, and she had overheard him. When Kilisinski found us awake, he was afraid he might not manage to kill all four of us, or that one of us might scream and a neighbour would hear. By the time he perfected his plot, we had gone. One positive outcome of the incident was that Luba learned that we were alive.

Still, we were out in the cold. "Where will we go now?" I demanded of Mother, since it was she who had insisted we leave. She suggested going to Wojtkowski, a rich farmer who lived not far away from the village. I was surprised, because his son had picketed our store in Grodzisk. "How can we trust them?" I asked. Mother answered, "Wladek's father picketed as well, but I doubt if Wladek would harm us, and I still prefer to trust a man like Wojtkowski, who is a genuine aristocrat and was a good friend of Father's." There was something to Mother's argument. Wojtkowski was one of the people who had apologized to Father for his son's picketing of our store. Besides, we had no choice.

Wojtkowski was not too happy to see us, but he asked us to sit down and told his wife to feed us. That would be all, he warned. He could give us bread to take along, as much as we wanted, but he couldn't endanger his family by hiding us. At least he spoke to us like human beings. We could tell that his family was heartbroken by our situation. Even his son Mikodom, who had picketed our store, was quiet and sad.

I knew by this time that we all had lice. Chanale was constantly scratching her head. We hadn't changed our clothes even once since we had left our house. We hadn't had a chance to wash, not even our hands. Nobody had offered us water, and outside it was already very cold in the early Polish winter. I begged Wojtkowski's permission to take off Chanale's shawl. He allowed me that. But how painful it was to see that Chanale's head at the back, behind her ears, was all swollen and wet with blisters. I took off my woollen socks and put them under her shawl to make it warmer. Wojtkowski looked on and shook his head from side to side, as if to say, *Why are you breathing? It's no use. You have no way out. There's no chance you'll survive.*

Something boiled up in me. I turned to him and said, "Do you think, Pan Wojtkowski, that a Jewish mother has less love for her child than a gentile one?"

"Under these circumstances, I doubt if you have a chance," he answered. "Your child is sick. How can you avoid getting sick too? It is freezing outside."

I had my answer ready for him. "If only you would help us a little. I don't mean you personally, but all you Poles, our neighbours, people we went to school with, whom we saw every day, did business with. Now everybody turns their backs on us. We were born here; we grew up together. Now you people are helping the Germans kill us. Like the murder of that little boy in the Czarny forest — who do you think committed a greater crime, the Germans who killed that boy, or the man who dragged him to the Germans? Who will have to pay for that crime? And for all the crimes? The war will come to an end," I said, "even if I'm not around to see it. You will hear, and with shame, that Poland was the only country that helped the Germans. They bought you with our blood! Poland, who herself was in slavery for more than a hundred years under the Russian Tsar, is now selling herself for the price of Jewish lives. Who will pay for the crimes committed in the twentieth century?"

Mother then begged me to stop talking, saying that they would throw us out.

"They'll throw us out anyway," I said. "Let me at least tell them who they are before I die, that going to church does not make them good Christians."

I turned back to Wojtkowski. "Would Jesus tell you to drag Jewish men, women and children, babies and newborns, to their deaths? I attended many of your lessons in religion, and I know this is not what Jesus would want you to do. You should know one thing: for a hundred years, Pan Wojtkowski, you were hoping for your freedom, for your own country, but you are losing it now whether or not a few Jews survive. At least your conscience will be clean if you help us a little bit."

I saw that Wojtkowski was moved. Then he said, "How can I help you? If I hide you, I'll be killed myself if they find out."

I said, "Just keep your big barn unlocked. As you can see, it's already four weeks since the Jews from Semiatych were wiped out, but we are still alive. If we could only find kind people! We still have valuable things to give in exchange for a piece of bread or a corner in a barn."

Wojtkowski then told us that there were too many of us together. He had enough bread for all four of us, but poorer people, even if they wanted to help us, wouldn't be able to feed us. "Who can I separate from?" I wanted to know. "From my child? From my elderly mother?"

"From your husband," he said. "His chances will be better as a man alone than with the three of you."

It was not easy for me to convince Avrumeh, or for him to decide, to try our luck separately once again. Wojtkowski's daughter, who was visiting them at the time from Warsaw, told us that there were still Jews in the ghetto there, and that Jews with trades were still working for the Germans. As my husband had been the only electrician in Semiatych, we hoped he would be needed there. Then we thought that perhaps the Polish woman who lived in my father-in-law's house, who seemed to be nice, would help him. Maybe if Avrumeh signed a document that after the war the house would be hers, she would hide him. There was plenty of room there. Wojtkowski's son showed Avrumeh how to get to the main road leading to Semiatych. The rest of us were allowed to stay overnight in his barn, but we had to promise we would leave in the morning.

After Avrumeh left, I asked Wojtkowski for advice on where to go first. He told us that Theodore Wojciuk, a neighbour of his who had a farm, had hidden Soviet soldiers, escaped prisoners of war. Maybe he would do something for us, too. I knew Theodore very well; we had been in the same grade at school. But this was different — I was sure that he had helped Russians because he himself was Russian. But Wojtkowski told me that at least he was a good man and that I should try, and that I didn't have to be afraid that he would turn me in to the

Germans or anything like that. He told us how to get there and agreed that we could stay one more day and leave the next day at sunset.

Mother spent the day crying. It was as if a stream had opened in her eyes and the tears were flowing. She couldn't forgive herself. Why hadn't that German killed her along with Father? "What kind of wife and mother are you to tell your husband to go alone when you have a small child?" she scolded me, and then blamed herself, saying that she was the reason that I had told my husband to go off by himself, and that in wartime, if you separate once, you may never find each other again. I answered that it was better for Avrumeh to be by himself, if that improved his chances of survival, than to die with us.

Throughout the day, Chanale kept herself busy opening pea pods that she found in the straw. Before the sun set, Wojtkowski came into the barn with bread and butter. He looked pale and sad. I could see he hadn't slept and that it was hard for him to ask us to leave.

Mother and I had the feeling that this day would be our last.

Risk and Reunions

When we reached Theodore Wojciuk's farm, I saw through the window that they had visitors, but I didn't recognize them. We went to a little sty near a very large barn and waited for the visitors to leave. Chanale slept in my lap. Looking around, Mother and I saw a big stack of hay in the yard. I would have gladly crawled into the pile without showing myself to Theodore. The pile would probably be there all winter. But Mother said we would freeze there.

Before we could decide on any course of action, we saw two men walking out of the house with a lantern, coming straight toward us. They were too near for us to hide or run from. But they were frightened too, and they demanded to know who we were.

I answered, crying, "Don't you see? Here is a desperate mother who wants to save her child. I escaped from the Germans. Please help me. You must have children of your own. What would you do in my place?"

Now I could tell that it was Theodore and his brother-in-law, whom I also knew very well. He turned to Theodore and said, "Oh, this is Rachela, from Grodzisk. Theodore, take them into the house. Look what's happened to them. If I lived on a farm, I would help them myself."

Theodore said that he couldn't let us stay because he was already known to the Germans for hiding Soviet prisoners of war. As we realized later, he didn't want his brother-in-law to see that he was inviting us into the house. During those times, a person couldn't trust anyone. When his brother-in-law left, Theodore called us to the house but told us in advance that we could only stay till morning. I begged him to let us stay in that big stack of hay or in the barn for at least a few days. But he explained that he had people working for him, and it would be dangerous. In the meantime, we could go into the house to warm up and eat.

Theodore and his wife had two children about the same age as Chanale. His wife, whom I knew, cried when she saw us, as had Theodore. I saw that the man was racked by sorrow and was asking himself how he could help us. I told him that we had many valuable goods, and maybe he could think of somebody who would hide us.

After a while, he told us that he had run into Klemens, who was very sorry about what had happened to our father's family. Klemens had told him that if my father, Ephraim, or his son Shaiko (Shieh's Polish name) escaped, he would hide them. "Klemens is always short of money," Theodore said, "and you have things to give. Maybe he has heard that you escaped and was hinting so that I should pass on the message if I saw you."

We spent the night in Theodore's house. I couldn't sleep. I was so relieved to learn that someone was willing to help us. But why had I told Avrumeh to try his chances alone, now that we might all be able to hide together? Before the sun rose, Theodore told us to get ready. He and his wife gave us a hot breakfast, and then he took us into a thick forest, to a cluster of three evergreen bushes. He started a small fire and then left to set out to talk to Klemens, telling us that he would come back at sunset and let us know what he could do for us.

After a few hours, the fire went out. Mother became very nervous and started to worry that Theodore would never show up, that he had brought us here only to get rid of us. She was also getting very cold. Her hands, and especially her injured arm, were freezing. I tried to rub them and did what I could, but I felt that I had to get

Mother warmed up. Since I knew that I wouldn't be able to find Theodore's place, I decided to try another house. We walked to the edge of that small forest, where I saw a very little house. Telling Mother to wait with Chanale, I started toward it with the intention of asking for warm water or matches to make a fire. A woman saw me through the window and recognized me as Jewish. She burst out of the house screaming, "What are you doing here? You should be dead by now. How come you are still alive?" I ran back to Mother and Chanale as quickly as my legs would carry me, afraid that maybe someone might chase and catch us. I knew by then what people were capable of.

When we were further back inside the forest, we couldn't find the place where Theodore had left us. I was angry with Mother. If Theodore returned, he wouldn't find us, and everything would be lost. Chanale was falling asleep. I sat down on the frozen earth and took her in my lap to protect her from freezing. Mother was pacing back and forth, wringing her hands and crying. Then she turned to me and said, "Listen to me, my child. We can't go on like this anymore. Let's go to Grodzisk and let the Germans shoot us. Let there be an end to all our suffering."

I said, "Please Mother, don't mention the Germans to me. I should go to them to be shot? I'd rather freeze here with Chanale on my lap. And please walk faster, maybe you'll warm up."

"What strength drives you on to live!" she exclaimed. "But what false hope! Can't you see that every day we are driven to another place? The war zone is very far, somewhere near Stalingrad, and it is December."

After some time, we heard footsteps. We hoped we would not be seen, but a man appeared from between the trees right in front of us. It was Niminski on his way to Grodzisk for church, so it must have been Sunday. He asked about Avrumeh. I told him that we had separated in the hopes that he would have a better chance alone, but that now we had nowhere to go. Mother asked him what he thought — did we have a chance? He answered that if we had found places to hide up to now, we might be lucky enough to find other ones. We should try, he urged us, though he couldn't hide us himself. He gave us matches, helped us make a small fire deeper in the woods and promised he'd pray for us in church. As he walked away, we saw him take out a handkerchief and wipe his eyes.

We warmed up a bit by the fire. Then I told Mother that we would have to go and find the spot where Theodore had left us, in case he came back to look for us. Mother didn't want to leave the fire, afraid she would freeze. I told her that if we couldn't find the spot, we would try to find his farm and hide in the haystack in the yard for a few days. We walked and walked but couldn't find the three evergreen bushes where Theodore had left us. Finally, it began to grow dark and we had to leave the woods because we couldn't see anything.

Once out of the brush, we saw a man looking around. It was Theodore, angry that we had left. "I have a place for you to hide!" he said. "Klemens told me to bring you. I think it's a good place, as long as you have something to pay him with." I grabbed his hands to kiss them, but he wouldn't let me. "You know I always admired you and looked up to you," he said, "and now you want to kiss my hands? It is everybody's duty to help his neighbour."

Theodore showed us to a very large stable on Klemens's farm. Inside, the stable was partitioned for pigs, cows, sheep and horses. It felt warm and heavenly. Soon Klemens arrived. He told us how sorry he was about what had happened to us, and he showed us to the loft of the barn. It was huge, as long as the barn itself. Wood was piled up on one side and on the other there was plenty of straw. We made ourselves a place to sleep in the straw. Klemens brought us supper and Mother gave him the money she had. Mother and Chanale fell asleep, but I lay awake anxiously. Why had I told Avrumeh to go alone? We could have been together here. Now who knows what would happen to him? The next day also passed in grief and sorrow, with Mother blaming herself for letting my husband strike out on his own.

The following day, just before midnight, we heard someone

climbing up the ladder to the loft. We were afraid that Klemens, or someone else who knew we were there, wanted to kill us. It was Klemens, but he had come to announce, "You'll never guess who's here! Your sister and her husband and son." It goes without saying that we were very happy to see them. But how on earth had they known we were here?

It turned out that they hadn't. A few hours after Mother had left Zalewski, who promised to hide Henia and her family, he turned them out, as well, and with this send-off to Henia: "Don't try to find anyone to hide you; no one will. If you can't face the Germans shooting you, the easiest death is to freeze. It's very cold outside. Take your family and go into the woods. Sit down on the frozen earth, and you'll fall asleep and freeze. That's the easiest way."

Henia couldn't believe her ears and just stared at him. Then he ordered her to take off her new sheepskin coat, which he had returned the day before along with other belongings she had given him for safekeeping. It would take longer to freeze in her new, warm sheepskin, he informed them. He would give her an old coat instead. Henia asked him if he really meant what he said or if he just wanted to scare them.

"I mean it," he answered. "You have no chance of surviving, so why shouldn't all your things remain with me?"

"Just try to take my coat," Henia retorted, "and I'll scratch your eyes out with my nails." But seeing that he was ready to fight, they ran away, leaving behind clothes, linens, furs and the other things Henia had trusted him to save for her, for the day she would need them to trade for bread, for one more day of life.

Who could figure these people out? When they came for our things, they were kind and sweet as honey. But how quickly they showed themselves to be snakes and murderers! Without our possessions we had nothing to offer, and pity was very hard to find.

Henia and her family had been driven from one place to another and, like my mother, Henia's son, Shieleh, had suggested going to

Semiatych to the Germans and getting it over with. Henia hoped that if she could only reach her good friend Theodore, who had helped her before, that he would save her once again. It was on the way to Semiatych, where Theodore lived, that she happened to knock on Klemens's door to beg for some water and to ask if they were on the right road.

There was no end to our joy on seeing each other, and Klemens agreed to let them stay with us. A few days later, though, he brought us bad news along with our breakfast. "I think your husband has been found dead," he told us. A Jew of around thirty had been shot on a road near Aleksandrowo. The man's appearance matched the description I had given him of Avrumeh, and as it was logical for Avrumeh to have been looking for us around here, we could only assume that Klemens was right. After all, I couldn't go and identify the body. It felt like a giant stone was pressing down on our hearts. Mother again blamed herself for letting him go off alone, and I, of course, blamed myself.

We begged Klemens to try and find out something about Shieh, but he said that if Shaiko hadn't shown up at his house by now, he probably wasn't alive.

Then he asked what else we had to give him. He too wanted Avrumeh's black suit, but we wanted to save it in case we had to go back to Wladek's. We told him that we would go get something for him but pleaded with him to give us two more days for me to get over the shock of his news about Avrumeh. He agreed to wait till Saturday evening. Since the stable was locked at night, he had to come and unlock it to let us out. When he arrived, he told us that a fierce storm was blowing, and it would be a sin to let even a mad dog go outside in this weather. He didn't have the heart to send us out and we, for our part, were glad for another day of shelter.

On Sunday it was no better outside, but this time Klemens said that he thought that perhaps it was better for us to go in stormy weather, as we were almost certain not to meet anybody. Henia and

I set out to Mikolai's for some of the possessions that I had there. Mother was heartbroken to watch us leave. Again, we were separated. But we had no choice — we had to give Klemens what he wanted.

When we stepped out of the stable, a gust of wet snow blew right into our faces. A few steps further I fell into a ditch and got wet up to my waist. Henia wanted to go back, but I insisted we reach Mikolai's. If we returned empty-handed Klemens would make us leave. Well, at least he was right about not meeting anybody in weather like this. Who in the world would risk going out in such a storm? It was really impossible to walk. We couldn't see the road. Snow and wind were blowing straight into our faces. Several times, we fell into ditches on one side of the road or the other. When we reached Mikolai's house we were both so wet and cold that we stopped for a moment to catch our breath. Lights shone through all the windows, and a marvellous smell of fried hamburgers wafted from the house. *People are still living normal lives*, I thought as I knocked on the door.

"Who is it?" Vera called.

"Rachela," I responded, using my Polish name.

She didn't answer and turned the lights down. Through the keyhole I told her that I hadn't come to stay. I only wanted to warm up and to pick up some of my belongings. She didn't answer. I begged and begged, but she didn't open the door or say a word. Then we waited quietly, trying to hear if Mikolai was at home. We heard Vera's mother, who must have been visiting from Grodzisk, say, "How can you do this to Rachela? She was your best friend. Please do this for me! I'm afraid God will punish us. If you don't want her in the house, at least give her what belongs to her." Vera didn't move. I knew that we couldn't go back to Klemens without anything. If he turned us out, we had nowhere else to go in this blizzard. I was determined not to let Vera get away with this. If pleading didn't work, maybe frightening her would.

"Don't think that I'm going to walk away from here with nothing and let you enjoy what belongs to me," I told her. "Before a German kills me, I'll see to it that he shoots you too. I'll know what to tell him. I myself will come back and burn your house down if you don't give me my clothes. They're worth my life! It's my life and Chanale's life that I buy with that clothing!"

But she still didn't answer. In desperation, I started to tear the hair from my head. Then Henia heard someone coming in our direction. Germans, we thought, though we knew that Germans rarely left their barracks after dark. We quickly smoothed out the snow where we had been standing and hid ourselves behind a bush. Peeking out, we saw Mikolai.

When he approached the gate to his house, I jumped out at him, crying, and started to tell him about his wife's reaction to me. He put his hand on my head. "Please calm down," he said, "I have two important things to tell you. Your husband was here in the morning. Vera chased him out, and he went in the direction of Aleksandrowo."

I was trembling and couldn't say a word. Henia said, "You had two things to tell us. What's the second one?"

"Your brother Shaiko was here a few hours ago with two young men, and when I told him where your husband went, he said he'd go look for him." Henia and I both jumped up to hug him. Tearfully, he said, "If my wife weren't so nervous, I would help you much more."

I didn't try to tell him that it was cruelty, not nerves. If she had only told me that my husband and brother had been there! If I had left without meeting Mikolai, how would we ever have found out they were still alive? And who knows if we would ever have found each other again? I pleaded with Mikolai to give me the black suit or some of our linens, telling him that we could not go back to where we were hiding without anything, for fear of being thrown out.

Mikolai told us to wait in the pigsty. It took him quite a while to come back, and when he did, it wasn't with the black suit, but with only two comforter covers. I didn't argue. I knew that if I returned to Klemens with the news that Shieh was alive, he would wait to see him. We warmed up a little in the sty, near the pigs, waiting for the storm to subside.

We were elated by the news that Avrumeh and Shieh were both alive. We hoped that Shieh had been able to hide his wife, Chana, and their two daughters somewhere, since Mikolai hadn't mentioned them. Our minds racing with ideas of how to locate my brother and husband, we decided to stop off at Wojtkowski's barn on our return to see if they were there. Knowing they were alive gave us strength to run. We knew how many kilometres we had to cover that night.

In Wojtkowski's barn, nobody answered when we called their names. We looked in the place where we had slept. When we shut the barn door, a dog near the house started to bark. We ran away and decided to go over to Wladek's, where we had been hidden for ten days. We quickly opened his barn door and looked around. There was so little hay that it wasn't hard to see that no one was there.

After talking it over, Henia and I decided to knock on the door to the house. Crouching under the window, we first listened to try and hear any noise. I thought I heard whispering, and the more I listened, the more certain I became that it was in Yiddish. Gently, I knocked on the window. Silence. I waited and knocked again. Nobody answered. I stood there in front of the window and said, "Please open the door. It's Ephraim's daughter from Grodzisk. I only want to find out about my husband."

Someone looked through the window to make sure I was telling the truth, then told me to come to the door. Wladek opened it, and there was Avrumeh standing behind him! Shieh and two young men, Chaim Marmur and Chazkel Rosenzweig, were all inside. When I threw my arms around Shieh, I could feel that he was sobbing. I didn't ask about his family; I knew what he was crying about. We talked for a little while, but we knew that it was still quite a distance to Klemens's barn, and Mother was waiting for us. Shieh told us that they would go back to where they were hiding and he would see us one evening toward the end of the week.

Henia, Avrumeh and I went back to Klemens's barn. I ran to Mother and cried, "Mama, Shieh is alive!" At first, she couldn't say a word. Then she asked me how I had heard about him, and when I told her I had seen him, she was visibly relieved.

Avrumeh told us that after he had left us, he walked till he felt very tired, and when he neared a cemetery, he decided that it would be the safest place to rest. He fell asleep, and when he woke up it was too light out to walk on the road, as someone might recognize him. He looked Jewish, especially after not having shaved for so long. So he hid in the cemetery till the sun set.

When he reached Semiatych, people were not yet asleep. First, he knocked on the door of his father's house. The woman who lived there had shown so much kindness when my father-in-law had worked for the Germans that we had assumed she would help. But when she opened the door and saw Avrumeh, it was as if she had seen a ghost.

"How dare you come here?" she burst out screaming. "Your father gave me the house, and you have no right to come here. If you don't go away, I'll call the Germans!"

As the German offices were a few blocks away, he couldn't risk staying even a minute, even though the lamps were on in the streets. Then he remembered two Polish sisters, one a widow with a son of nine and the other who was single. They lived with their mother and younger brother. Both women worked for the Germans in the office where he had worked as an electrician, and they used to come to our house to buy radios and electrical appliances. He decided to try them, even though he had to cross through the centre of the town under the bright lamplight. He was lucky that when he knocked on their door, the young widow opened it. She let him into the cellar, warning him first that her mother wouldn't approve, and second, that she and her sister were expecting German visitors. Without much time to think, he slipped into the cellar only a short while before two Germans arrived. They and the girls talked, drank, danced and had a good time practically right over his head.

The scene repeated itself for several evenings. On the whole, though, things were pretty good, and the young women brought him food. But one day the widow's little boy went into the cellar to look for something, found Avrumeh there and told his grandmother, who was furious. When the young women returned from work, their mother told them that Avrumeh would have to go. They and their teenage brother cried and begged her to let him stay. They were the last ones people would suspect, the women argued. But their mother threatened to inform the Germans if he didn't leave. The teenaged son walked with Avrumeh through the city so that he would be less conspicuous and gave him some cigarettes, apologizing for his mother's behaviour.

Avrumeh walked the eighteen kilometres to Mikolai's all in one night, arriving so exhausted that he went straight to the barn and fell asleep. When Vera came to the barn, she heard heavy breathing and, thinking a wild animal had got in, ran and called a neighbour. The neighbour arrived with an iron pitchfork and started to poke at him. When Vera realized who it was, she made a bigger fuss than if she had really discovered a wild animal! Avrumeh then ran to Wladek's, where we met him.

In the morning, when Klemens came, we gave him the two comforter covers and told him that we had been so excited about finding Avrumeh and Shieh that we hadn't waited to get the other things. We told him that Shieh would come the following week. The news about Shieh, or Shaiko, as Klemens called him, was more than enough to make him happy. He started to dream about what Shaiko could do for him, and he gave us a whole list of things he needed. The first item was more flour for bread. He had his own family of ten, and now we seven had been added. But what Klemens didn't know was that Shaiko was no longer the person he had been in Grodzisk when he owned the dairy and had given Klemens whatever he needed, from seeds to farm machinery, and allowed him to pay up slowly. How in the world could Shieh get supplies now? He had only the clothes on his back and a little money. Unlike us, he had not had the chance to leave clothes, furs and linens with gentiles, although, when we had asked people to store these things, we hadn't realized that it would be so hard to get them back.

When we met at Wladek's, Shieh, Chaim and Chazkel were already realizing what a mistake they had made by not taking more valuables along with them to exchange for food or a corner in a stable. Henia and I suggested that now with his and the young men's help, we could retrieve the things we had given to Mikolai and Zalewski for safekeeping, and we all agreed that any one of us who had something to barter would share the benefits with the others.

In Klemens's barn, every day that passed felt like a year, especially till evening arrived and we could be sure that the Germans wouldn't come anymore. But each day that we waited for Shieh was like a century.

Many days later, Shieh returned with the two young men. Chazkel hoped that maybe we had news of his father, Mr. Rosenzweig, the head of the Judenrat, but we had neither seen nor heard of him after we walked out of that forest near Semiatych. His mother and his sister Ruzka, he found out, had reached the village of Tolwin, but there, a German they knew from Semiatych had shot them with one bullet while the mother and daughter embraced.

Shieh told us that there had been a rumour in the ghetto that Avrumeh, Chanale and I had been shot to death outside the ghetto. My mother-in-law had wept, and Shieh, too, had believed it, and had thought we were dead.

Then Shieh told us what had happened to him on the night of November 2, when we escaped from the ghetto. When he and his family heard the shooting, they ran out of their house and managed to get as far as Deitsch's factory. Shieh, his wife, Chana, and their two daughters crawled under a large pile of chopped wood in the factory yard. They planned to wait there until the next night and then try to get out of the ghetto, but the factory janitor, Josef, was searching for Jews and found the family. He pulled them out of their hiding place and beat up Shieh so badly that he couldn't even stand. Chana and the children had to drag him back to the house.

The next day Shieh could walk, and they all moved over to the part of the ghetto where we had lived, taking with them dry bread, blankets and other things, in the hope that they would be able to hide in the double wall we had built in our attic until they could see what was going on with the other Jews. They were in there for two days when their younger daughter, Yentale, started to cry that she didn't want to sit there anymore but wanted to play with the children she saw through the cracks in the wall. They tried to comfort her and explain, but it didn't help. She cried constantly. Finally, on the third day, Chana couldn't take it anymore and begged Shieh to agree to go downstairs, saying that what had happened to everybody would happen to them. Shieh's friends were surprised and told him so. They didn't expect to see him, of all people, still sitting in the ghetto. He knew so many gentiles in and around Semiatych. Some of his friends even offered to give him jewellery and money to help him escape. But every day, people who had managed to escape in the beginning came back to the ghetto, some brought in by gentiles and some of their own free will because they couldn't find a place to hide and were cold and hungry. Seeing this, Shieh gave up. Maybe some others did as well.

On Monday, November 9, the first group of Jews was taken to the train station that was seven kilometres from Semiatych. The order had gone out to the farmers to come with their horses and carriages, and Shieh saw the way the Jews were taken to the trains — dragged out of their houses and driven there like animals. How they were shoved into the carriages was shameful to see. Old people and sick people who couldn't walk were dumped into the carriages like pieces of dirt. Among them was Avrumeh's whole family.

After Shieh told us this, we begged him to change the subject. It was more than enough for one evening. Shieh was lucky not to have been in the first transport and to have had time to plan his escape, but he had not been able to convince his wife and two daughters to stay hidden and escape with him. He would not speak any more about them.

Shieh and the young men had very little with them, and, like us, they had to pay for their hiding place, which we learned was at Marya's in the village of Kłopoty-Bańki. We started to discuss how we would get our belongings. Shieh suggested going back to the ghetto, where he had buried four large metal boxes full of all kinds of clothing and linens. The boxes were hidden along the path to the house, four paces from the door and nine paces from a fence. The work had been done extremely well, and Shieh assured us that nobody would think of digging there. Chaim and Chazkel were enthusiastic, and they started to talk about who else to ask for help and the optimal time for this operation. Our cousin Moniek Goldshtern had also escaped from the ghetto and was somewhere in the area. Moniek was young and strong, exactly the man they needed for the job, and when Shieh managed to find him, he agreed to help. Shieh proposed that the best times would be Christmas Eve or New Year's Eve, when people would be a bit drunk and sleep more soundly.

Meanwhile, the sores on Chanale's head had become worse and now spread over her whole scalp. Her hair had gotten so sticky that we had to cut it off. It was a pity to see the way the child suffered. Even in her sleep she would rub her head on the straw we used for pillows. I couldn't ask Klemens for medicine, since we were afraid that if he knew about Chanale's condition, he would get scared that his children would get it too. Mother cried a lot about how Chanale looked. She remembered how proud she had always been to take her granddaughter to her good friend Ruchl Steinberg's on Saturday afternoons, how everybody had admired the child, who had always been dressed beautifully, and how Chanale's long black hair under her white angora hat had made her look even more beautiful. "What has become of her?" Mother repeated again and again. "How can we cry about the dead when we see that it is so much worse for the living?"

Once, when we were talking about our family and other people dear to us, Mother mentioned the word lonesome, and Chanale burst out crying. "This is the word I wanted to tell you!" she exclaimed. "That I'm lonesome for all those people who were with us before and now I can't see them anymore." She started to recite all their names, and told us that when she closed her eyes, she saw them, but when she opened her eyes, they disappeared. We realized then how much our little girl, like us, missed all the people we had left in the ghetto.

We waited anxiously for Shieh's weekly visits. We knew that he was still planning to dig up the boxes that he and the families who had lived with him had buried in front of their house. By then, the gentiles who had lived in the area of the ghetto had returned to live in their houses. We all knew how dangerous the expedition would be, but there was no choice. We had little chance of surviving, but without those goods we had even less. We were anxious every time we thought about it — imagine digging right in front of a house where people were living! Everyone except Mother knew the job was scheduled for Christmas Eve. The days before that risky expedition were almost impossible to get through.

Finally, a couple of days after Christmas Eve, Shieh and the boys arrived, successfully loaded down with sheepskin coats and other things that were very valuable at the time. Shieh, in the end, had not actually gone into town. The others hadn't wanted him to, telling him that nobody was left to cry over them if they were killed, since their families were all dead, but that Shieh still had a family, and they knew we would be lost without him. So Shieh remained hidden on a nearby farm instead and then helped to bring back the items.

We eventually heard how shocked the neighbours and the whole police force were by what the young men had done, and that by the next day the whole town was talking about it. They'd figured out that it was Shieh's doing because there was hardly a spot in the former ghetto where people had not already searched and dug for goods that Jews had buried, and no one else would have known where those boxes were. A few weeks later the men went back to the ghetto, this time to the place where Chaim Marmur had lived, and they brought clothes from there as well. But when they tried a third time, they were chased and almost lost their lives. After that, they didn't go back.

As for Klemens, he naturally talked differently about hiding us when he saw what Shieh had to offer him in exchange. Shieh had managed to sell some of the items and gave Klemens flour for bread, seeds for his fields and clothes for his wife and children.

Shieh gave me a short sheepskin coat and for Chanale, a grey sheepskin coat that had been made for Yasha, Mr. Fishelson's daughter, who had never worn it. Later we realized that without it Chanale would have frozen, but at the time it tortured me to see her in that coat — every time I looked at it, I saw little Yasha's face and her blond, wavy hair.

Safe and Thankful

Time was passing, even under those conditions. Klemens brought us hopeful news, that people around the railway station in Semiatych had seen trains returning from the Soviet Union with frozen-looking Germans inside. In the country where Napoleon had met the beginning of his end, history was now repeating itself for the Germans.

But in the meantime, for us, with the coming of spring, we had more fleas and lice to cope with. Without water to wash, it was impossible for us to deal with all the insects, and at night we had to fight the mice and rats too. We couldn't leave the stable, since Klemens's younger children didn't know about us, and his house was the first one on the main road, where many people passed.

One sunny day in March 1943, Shieh came to see us. Klemens, wanting to give us a break from our shelter, told us to go down where all his animals were and to flatten out the manure. We worked there till the afternoon, when Klemens brought us something to eat and we went back up to the loft. Because we had come from downstairs, we ate in the open, not in our usual hiding place in the straw. When we finished, everyone except Chanale, Mother and I went to the hiding place in the straw.

Then I heard the barn door open with a bang and my heart started to race. As I put a finger to my lips, a sign that we had to be absolutely silent, I heard people coming into the barn, speaking in German.

Somebody must have betrayed us. I was just about to climb down the ladder to give myself away and thus try to save the others when I heard them counting the pigs, and then they walked out. I went back to our hiding place, and we waited for Klemens.

When he came up, he said, "You're lucky that the Germans didn't give me a chance to say anything! I wanted to tell them that you had come last night and that I just found you, but they screamed at me not to talk. When I saw one of them pointing at the pigs, I realized that they had come for the pigs and not for you." He repeated again and again how lucky we were that they hadn't given him a chance to say what he had planned to.

When he left, Shieh said, "How can we trust him now? How close we all were to being shot! I'll have to try to find another place for you." But we all knew how hard it would be to find a safer place.

One day in April, there was a hunt for Jews in the village of Morze. The Germans had been told that at night, many Jews begged for food in and around that village, and that some of them were being hidden by the farmers. A few Jews had been tipped off to stay away from the village and the whole area while the Germans were on the prowl. Some Jews escaped from the area, but one Jew from Ciechanowiec was killed.

Very early one morning, a man named Konstanty Krynski, who lived on a farm not far from Morze, saw two German soldiers and a young man walking toward his farm. Two Jewish girls from Semiatych, Doba and Luba Marmur, cousins of Chaim Marmur, were hidden in his house. On seeing the Germans, Krynski went outside and started to chop wood. When the Germans approached and asked whether he was harbouring any Jews, he responded with a resounding "No!" and, happening at just that moment to spot a Jewish boy running through the fields some distance away — too far for the Germans to catch — he pointed excitedly. "There's a Jew! There's a Jew!" That's how he got rid of the Germans and saved the two sisters — for the time being. Shieh, who had contact with the girls, told us that they had moved on to another hiding place but still considered the Krynskis to be the best people in the world and from time to time went to visit them.

Klemens was not the same after the Germans came to count his pigs. He lost all hope that he could keep us safe until the end of the war. Over the course of the winter, he had tried to extort more and more payments for hiding us. Now though, he began to come up with stories about the war and how it wasn't going to end so soon, and repeatedly told us that he was too nervous to hide us any longer.

On May 10, 1943, Klemens finally climbed up to the loft and said that we had to go. He just couldn't stand it anymore. We knew then that Jews were meeting at night in the woods around the villages of Krynki-Sobole and Kłopoty-Bańki. Now that it was warmer, some of them even slept in the woods. Henia decided that she and her husband and son, who was almost twelve now, would try to hide in the woods too. I talked Klemens into letting me stay till the next time Shieh came. I knew that I couldn't manage in the woods with Chanale and Mother, who was very weak. Mother's arm had healed, but after just lying and sitting in the loft all winter, she couldn't walk. I promised Klemens that we'd hide in the loft so well that even he wouldn't be able to find us.

Henia and her family left that night. Avrumeh and I arranged the lumber in the loft so that most of the floor was empty, and then the four of us crawled into the space we had left behind the wood and waited. When Klemens arrived, he couldn't find us till we answered his call. Still he wanted us to leave. We begged him to just let us wait for Shieh, who we hoped would come that same evening.

When Shieh did come for us that night, Klemens didn't want to hear about letting us stay any longer. Shieh begged him to give him time to find another place.

On the following evening, May 11, 1943, the Germans conducted a massive hunt for Jews in Kłopoty-Bańki, following leads from an informer. Luba Marmur had been shot dead — Luba, a beautiful eighteen-year-old girl, who was very much in love with Chazkel, who was also eighteen. Love doesn't wait for the right conditions, especially not at eighteen, and from time to time they had been able to meet at night in the woods around Krynki-Sobole. That evening, Luba had asked Moniek Goldshtern to take her to Chazkel's hiding place. As we later learned, she had stopped by the Krynskis' house to wash and to make herself more beautiful. She sang and danced, and before she stepped out of the door, she even put a red flower in her black hair. From Krynski's they went to the barn, but not finding Chazkel or the others, they walked on slowly between the stables. Then, from behind one of the stables, a shot rang out. Moniek had managed to escape to the woods.

By morning the whole district knew what had happened. People came to look at Luba, beautiful even after she was killed.

Henia and her family, the same night they left, reached the forest near Krynki-Sobole but didn't find any Jews there. In the morning a young boy, a shepherd, saw them and came over. Henia later told me that she spoke to him, asking for shelter, but he didn't answer; he just looked at them and then ran away. Half an hour later, he returned with his older sister, Stasia, who remembered Henia and Sruleh from their store. She had been there a few times to look for a coat but had never had the money to buy one. Stasia remembered with fondness how my sister had let her have a coat for much less than the actual cost.

When Henia asked Stasia if they could stay in her barn for a few days, she said that she had to ask her three brothers, with whom she shared the house. In the evening, she returned with her brother Josef, who agreed to let them stay in their barn. But Krynki-Sobole was just a kilometre from Kłopoty-Bańki, where the next day the raid took place. This frightened Stasia and her brothers, and although they initially wanted Henia and her family to leave, they eventually agreed to take the risk and let them stay.

When Klemens, too, heard about the raid in Kłopoty-Bańki, he was adamant we leave. Shieh, Chaim and Chazkel, shocked and upset by the raid and Luba's death, brought us to Wojtkowski's barn and told him that somebody had promised to take us in, but that we had to wait a few days. Wojtkowski agreed to let us stay. His daughter, who lived in Warsaw, was also there and she told us that she couldn't bear to watch the ghetto burning with the Jews in it. We were surprised to hear that there were any Jews left in Warsaw by that time, for the newspapers had triumphantly announced that city had been made *judenrein* — "cleansed" of Jews — and that Jews found hiding were immediately executed along with the people who gave them shelter.

In the meantime, Shieh, after running around asking people to hide us, finally found Panie Boguszewska, who was willing to take us in for two weeks. We moved into a very small attic in her shabby barn. One side of the attic had a wooden wall with many cracks in it, which in the daytime, let in enough light for us to be able to do some handiwork. Panie Boguszewska gave me some navy-blue wool to make a sweater for her daughter. At the end of a week I had finished the sweater and trimmed it with white angora wool. It was very beautiful, and when her daughter wore it to church, she received many compliments. Panie Boguszewska told everyone that she had knitted it herself. Naturally, she was thrilled, and she asked me if I could do other things. The following week, I crocheted a white woollen shawl, which she also wore to church. With the sweater and shawl, Panie Boguszewska forgot that she had given us only two weeks to stay. Mother started knitting gloves for her family, and I made all kinds of sweaters, which she sold.

At Panie Boguszewska's we regained our strength. She fed us better than Klemens had, and most importantly, she treated us like human beings. But the place was extremely cramped. There was only enough room for us to sit or lie down, but not to walk about much.

Our Chanale felt miserable. She was lonesome for little Shieleh, who she had played with when we were all together. Through the same cracks that let in the light for us to work by, she could see other children playing outside. The house and barn were in a village, and it was late spring, early summer, May and June, when everything grows and blossoms. Even the birds sang better in the spring. Well, during this time, Mother would tell Chanale all kinds of stories from the Bible and from Jewish history. All the stories had a happy ending for Jews, and Chanale constantly demanded, "When will that miracle happen to us? When will I be able to go outside and play with the children?" Her longing for the outside was unbearable. She envied the chickens she saw pecking at their food and the sheep she saw running in the fields — she wanted to be one of them — but, most of all, she wanted to be a bird. "The Germans wouldn't reach me. I would fly higher and higher. I would spit in their faces."

We tried to feed her on the hope that soon, soon our liberation would come. But we knew that freedom was a long way off. Though they were slowly retreating, the Germans were still deep in the Soviet Union.

By this point we had given away almost everything we had and were desperate to get our things back from Mikolai. Shieh and one of the young men went to ask for them, but Mikolai told them that Germans had searched his house and taken everything. Shieh knew that this was a lie, having asked one of the neighbours about it, so I asked Panie Boguszewska if she would take a letter and personally place it in Mikolai's hand when he left the office where he worked. She agreed.

I wrote a long letter reminding Mikolai of our family friendship. *You shouldn't be corrupted by the idea of possessing another suit or article of clothing,* I wrote. *You won't enjoy wearing them, knowing that those same things could have bought another few days or weeks of life for my family and me.* I also reminded him that there is such a thing as having to live with oneself, that no matter how he might try to forget the wrong he was doing, and it might be buried deep, it will never go away. I told him that he shouldn't let himself be influenced by his wife, who wanted our belongings, but should rather make her understand what they were doing to desperate, half-dead people. I reminded him how he had once told me with pride about his experiences in World War I, when he had warned Jewish families who were about to be robbed. I tried to make him understand that the world wouldn't come to an end after the war, and that whoever survived would have on his conscience every wrong he had done.

When Panie Boguszewska came back, she asked me what I had written to Mikolai. She told me that when he read the letter, he started to cry and didn't stop, even when he finished it. Then Mikolai told her, "No matter what, tell them to come for their things." A few evenings later, I went with Avrumeh and we got our belongings back.

~

People in the neighbourhood started to talk, saying that Panie Boguszewska might be hiding Jews. They didn't believe that she and her daughter had made all the sweaters and other things that she was showing off. Someone also noticed what they believed was an item a Jew had given her in return for shelter.

Shieh tried to convince the Krynskis, who had proven their trustworthiness with the Marmur girls, to take us in. At first, they didn't want to hear of it. But finally, they agreed to two weeks. Everyone was afraid to hide us with Mother, who was sixty-two but looked much older, and with Chanale. People just couldn't understand how a young child could be hidden and not cry out.

Panie Boguszewska was really sorry when we told her that we were going, but Shieh felt that the rumours that she was hiding Jews made it too risky to stay on. That kind and honest woman didn't understand the danger she and her family were in. We were also sorry to leave a place where somebody wanted us. Panie Boguszewska promised that she would let us stay in her stable if we came back.

The Krynskis greeted us warmly and gave us a corner in a loft of a shabby barn. They were poor people but very well-known in the district for their honesty. They had three children — a daughter named

Gienia, who was married and lived in the village and didn't know about us or the other Jews who had been coming and going; a son in his twenties, Heniek, and a twelve-year-old daughter, Krysia. The girl would come up to the loft after school; we helped her with her homework and then she played with Chanale. There, too, Mother and I knitted sweaters and sewed shirts by hand, trying to be useful.

At the end of the two weeks, old Krynski told us that they didn't have the heart to make us leave. They were all very religious and believed that if we had lived until now and had come to them, they shouldn't be the ones to throw us out.

"Besides," he said, "I was a prisoner in Germany during World War I, and I know what hunger means. You are facing death without ever having committed a crime. Who should we help? The Germans who grabbed our country and are destroying it? Or you? You don't know me, but after I got out of the German prison, I was poor, and your father used to lend me salt and fuel."

He told us about a time when he was in our store and wasn't able to pay, but didn't have the nerve to ask for something before he had paid for the items he had bought earlier. My father told him not to be shy and said, "We are only human. No one knows what will happen to himself the next day. Maybe someday I'll be poor, and I'll need your help." I suppose that Father wanted to make him feel better. He knew Krynski was an honest man and would pay us as soon as he had some money.

"Maybe God made your father be good to me," Krynski said, "so that I would help you now." So we remained there beyond the two promised weeks.

The Krynskis didn't have much to eat. But in the evenings, if a few hungry Jews came by when Krynski was about to take a pail of potatoes to feed his pigs, he would let the Jews have the potatoes and would let the pigs go hungry for a night. None of those Jews had anything to give him in exchange, nor did he ask anything of them.

When we had arrived, Krynski hadn't asked what he would get

for hiding us. In the beginning, he hid us as a way of repaying my father's kindness. But then, he and his family just didn't have the heart to turn us out. They were always satisfied with what Shieh gave them and never bargained. They always said, "The war isn't over yet. Make sure you have enough to help you to the end." I was very moved by Krynski's behaviour and his warm feelings for every living person, no matter their religion. He always said, "We are not here to judge and condemn people for what they believe. One thing I know — in every religion, killing is a crime." That simple uneducated farmer had more humanity and feeling for what was right than the whole German "master race"!

The summer months passed quickly and soon the fall winds started to blow into the loft. The nights were cold. We didn't have anything to cover ourselves with, and the Krynskis had nothing to spare. At Shieh's suggestion, Heniek Krynski, with Avrumeh's help, dug out a shelter for us under the stable. They put wood on top of it to make a floor, and they piled wheat and the rest of their harvest for the winter on top. A wooden shack stood next to the barn, and there the Krynskis kept the wood they had chopped for their stoves. In the floor of the shack, next to the wall of the barn, was an opening, big enough for one person to get through and slide into our new shelter. The opening to our hiding place was covered by a trap door made of a large wooden board with pieces of chopped wood nailed onto it. It looked like a real wood pile and we were able to cover ourselves without leaving any sign that we were there.

We felt safer there, and the Krynskis felt surer that they would be able to protect us till the end of the war. We promised they would get the reward they deserved for all their trouble and fear. There were many times when I felt sorry for them. Why should these kind, gentle people get involved in our tragedy? But on the other hand, how could I save my child if not with their help? There was only one answer — if even one of us lived through the war, we would never forget them. We kept reminding ourselves of this. Every day at sunset, when Krynski milked the cow, he would come to the little shack, cough twice as a signal, and give Chanale a glass of milk. Every time he did that, Mother urged me always to remember his kindness.

The hiding place under the shack, which I called our "palace," was big enough for five people to lie down in — four places for us and one for Shieh when he visited — and high enough to sit in. It was pitch black. After a few weeks, Shieh brought us a lamp so that we could do some handiwork. The Krynskis didn't have enough for us to eat, so Shieh brought me wool to knit sweaters, which he then exchanged for food. He, Chaim and Chazkel were with Henia and her family at the shelter she had found, which was about two kilometres away in Krynki-Sobole.

I called our new shelter a palace because we felt more secure there, but Mother called it being buried alive. We often had to open the wooden trap door a crack just to give us enough air to breathe. And because there wasn't enough air, we couldn't light the lamp whenever we wanted to either. But the tremendous will to live through the war — or was it the will to keep my child alive? — made me thankful for every hour that passed, because each one brought us nearer to the end of the war.

Krynski brought us newspapers whenever he could get them. We knew that the Germans were retreating. We were full of hope. But one day in October 1943, he came with the news that on a farm in Krynki-Sobole there had been another hunt for Jews, and that a boy of seventeen had been shot by a Polish youth. Krynki-Sobole was not only so close by, but also where the rest of our family was hiding, and we were shocked. The Krynskis were scared. But we felt even worse when, a few evenings later, Shieh told us that it was my mother's nephew, Shimon Goldshtern, who had been killed — and by whom? By a boy our cousin had gone to school with in Grodzisk!

Mother couldn't stop crying about Shimon — to be shot by a schoolmate after eleven months of torture and suffering! "If no one survives," she said, "how will the world know what has happened to us? There won't be anyone left to tell what the Germans and our Polish friends did to us." Mother didn't know yet that even if we did survive, very few would care to listen to our tragedy.

The days passed in sorrow and grief. We heard that the Soviets were moving forward, and we waited anxiously to see if they would cross the old Polish-Russian border, terribly afraid they would stop there. We had no hope that anyone else would liberate us. As Mother kept saying, "The whole world has become deaf to our suffering."

So Close to Freedom

One day in January 1944, Krynski brought us a newspaper that said that the Soviets had crossed the old Polish-Russian border and were slowly moving forward. It is hard to describe our happiness. I even grabbed Krynski to kiss him for the good news. He cried along with us, but this time we were all crying with joy and were full of hope that we would soon be liberated.

The Krynskis were a bit tired of us, too, having lived for so long in constant fear. Panie Krynska had begun to go to church more often and taught Chanale how to pray to God in her own way. Chanale made a deal with Mother, that she would pray first to our God and then to Krysia's. She said to Mother, "Can't you see, Bobeh, that two Gods can help us more than one?" Mother cried when she saw Chanale first recite all the Jewish prayers she had taught her, then kneel at the wall and say the Catholic prayers she had learned from Krysia and Panie Krynska.

One day at the beginning of February, Krynski slid into the shelter very nervously and said, "I had really hoped to hide you till the end of the war, but with what I saw today in Ostrożany, it doesn't look like I'll be able to." He was shaking so much that we were afraid to ask him what had happened. He told us that he had seen a man dragging a Jew by a chain. The Jew was Yudel Suchar, one of the nicest men in Ciechanowiec, a town about thirty kilometres from the Krynskis' farm. Yudel and his two brothers had owned a large grain mill, and Krynski used to go to Ciechanowiec and see Yudel, tall and handsome, managing the entire business. But in Ostrożany that day he had seen him helpless, his feet wrapped in rags, being dragged by a man half his size. Krynski waited all day to see what would happen. He saw a German hand a gun to the man who was dragging Yudel and order him to shoot him. Krynski stood there, watching that once rich and well-built man, whose looks and position he had so admired and envied, shot while in rags and chains.

Now Krynski wanted us to leave. But where would we go at this point, and in the winter? We worked hard to persuade him to let us stay. We promised not to open our shelter until late at night, when we would be sure that no one would see us.

We were hearing better and better news, that the Soviets were approaching Rovno (Rivne). They seemed so near, and it wouldn't take long before they liberated us. That hope gave us strength to hold on. Lying in the dark on the wet straw, we dreamed of and hoped for the day of liberation.

As the Red Army drew nearer, we heard that Polish nationalist underground groups were plotting to rid their country of the remaining Jews before it was too late. As often happens in wartime, evil constantly seemed to win. Decent people were afraid to speak their minds. These groups, some of whose members were rumoured to belong to the Polish Home Army, the Armia Krajowa, wanted a pure Polish country. They didn't risk their lives when they found and killed unarmed Jews, yet they considered themselves patriotic heroes. Young people are always eager to become heroes, and the groups grew and spread. The closer the Soviet army came, the harder these outlaws worked.

The underground groups, unlike the Germans, started hunting in the evenings. Krynski and Shieh informed us that these people were finding Jews in barns and killing them, then beating up the people who had sheltered them and confiscating all their valuables. These bandits could grab whatever they pleased, and the victims had nowhere to lodge a complaint; the Poles certainly couldn't complain to the German authorities about their stolen property or protest their violated rights. And for us, this plague of "patriots" was unbearable, especially when the Soviets were already in Poland and less than a few hundred kilometres away.

Sometimes the Krynskis would ask us to come into their house in the evening, but I would refuse, explaining that it was hard for Mother to get in and out of the shelter and I didn't want to leave her. Avrumeh, though, had often gone to keep them company in the evenings, and to straighten out his back.

One evening in May, Shieh stopped by and gave the Krynskis a few yards of cloth and other things so they would keep us another two weeks. The next evening, Avrumeh was at the Krynskis' house and returned around ten o'clock. As Shieh had also brought me wool for a sweater, I went on knitting by lamplight a bit longer. At midnight, we decided to go to sleep. We had trained our bowels to go only once in twenty-four hours, always before bed-time. Usually Mother went out first, then I would go and clean up so that no mark would be left. That evening, Mother felt very weak, and I wasn't sure if she would be able to find the spot we used for this purpose, so I went out first to find it for her, planning to go out again after everybody and clean up. The light was still on in the shelter. When I opened the cover to go out, I saw two men with rifles slung over their shoulders, one on each side of the house. Luckily, they had their backs turned at that moment, and I was able to replace the cover without being spotted. Once inside again, I fell onto the straw, trembling. Mother and Avrumeh realized that I had seen something terrible. I told them, "Everything is lost; bandits have surrounded the house. They will surely come here and find us." The only thing we had with us was a pocket watch; Avrumeh put it in the straw so that Krynski would find it someday. We held on to each other tightly and waited for them to rip open the entrance to our shelter. There was a tremendous wind that evening, and the door of the shack that led to our shelter kept opening and banging. Every time it banged, we thought that they were coming. Chanale, as young as she was, didn't cry; she shook with fear, just as we did.

Finally, the cover to our shelter opened and somebody slid in. I felt something give inside me. At first, we thought that it was one of them. Then I saw old Krynski, his face beaten up. We didn't know whether they had left, or he had come to call us out to be shot. None of us could say anything. Krynski was the first to speak. Some of the men had been in his house and had taken everything Shieh had given them the evening before. The cloth and the other things suggested to them that the Krynskis were hiding Jews. The other men beat up the old couple and demanded they show them where the Jews were. Then they searched for us in the stable, but fortunately, they didn't go to the little shack with the opening to our shelter.

Krynski cried bitterly, saying they just couldn't hide us till the end. They were too nervous and scared. He told us that the men had promised to come again, and how could he be sure they wouldn't find us the next time? And all their torment would be for nothing, he said. I could hardly find the words to talk to him. I felt sorry for him and his family, that they had become involved with us. I was almost sorry that the men hadn't found us and ended it all. If they were going to kill us anyway, did we really want to live through the horrible fear of this night all over again? Did we really want to be in this grave and wait for them?

But to Krynski I said, "Would you feel any better if we left and were killed tomorrow?" He said, "No, I don't want you to die. You have become a part of my family, but I am afraid everything will be wasted, your suffering and ours." It took us quite a while to calm him down. When he finally left, we all cried bitterly. Here was a new plague, and we didn't know what to do about it.

The next day we mentioned to Panie Krynska that we were thinking of trying to find another place to hide and she told us, "If you think that you can survive somewhere else, try. We are willing to keep you until your liberation, and I believe that God will help us. But it is up to you."

We were overwhelmed by her words. The Krynskis, free people, were willing to share our destiny. Mulling this over, we decided to remain. We didn't know where it would be safer, but we did know that we couldn't find nicer people than the Krynskis. So we covered the entrance to our shelter better, Avrumeh didn't visit the house any-more, and we paid close attention to every noise outside. With the passing of the winter, almost everything in the barn had been used up and only a small amount of hay was left to cover the wood that formed our roof, so we could hear everything that happened in the barn very well.

Once, Krysia came down to the shelter coughing. When she left, Mother worried that she had the whooping cough and that Chanale would catch it from her. But how could we tell Krysia not to come? For one thing, Chanale so much wanted to see her; though Krysia was much older, Chanale had found a playmate in her. For another, we weren't in a position to give orders. After a few visits, Chanale started to cough too, and it did turn out to be whooping cough. We were desperate. If any of those bandits showed up, they would hear her.

One night we heard the barn door open and somebody walk in and then lay down. We held our breaths. We knew that there was a drunkard in the district, and we thought that he might have come in to pass the night. But, then again, the intruder might be one of the nationalists, come to keep an eye on the farm.

Chanale started to cough, and I grabbed a rag and covered her mouth. She began to choke. I had heard about babies who had choked when their mothers had tried to put something over their mouths to keep them quiet. I was terrified. Then, while Chanale was still gasping for breath, I heard someone at the lid of the shelter. I froze with fear, but a second later I saw Shieh's face there. Before he had a chance to say one word, I pushed Chanale into his arms and whispered, "Run quickly!" Avrumeh ran out after them. They went to the bushes in the fields. I had to stay because Mother was too weak to run and also because she would talk in her sleep. When Mother was awake, Chanale and I never let her cry very much. Chanale used to say to her, "Bobeh, I don't like your crying face, I like it better when you tell me stories." So she let out all the bitterness in her sleep. I had to wake her every few minutes.

Heniek Krynski heard something happening around the barn and came to see what it was. Again, I heard the barn door open, and my heart sank. Knowing that we would be frightened, he started to talk, asking who was there. Our visitor turned out to be the drunkard, after all. Though he was less threatening than the bandits, his knowing about us could also be dangerous, so Heniek kept him company through the night and in the morning, took him up to the house. Avrumeh, Shieh and Chanale came back in the evening. In the fields, Chanale had felt much better.

Two weeks later Krynski brought us the news that the Soviets were approaching Semiatych and that Germans had been seen running away, without their caps and without their weapons. This was the sweetest moment of our lives. A few days later we heard heavy shooting and the constant noise of airplane engines. Our hearts started to beat faster. At night, when we looked out and saw fires in the direction the Soviets were expected to come from, we realized that the front was coming very near.

I started to think about the night we had escaped from the ghetto. What had made me run out of the house without waiting for my father to come down from the attic? I thought it was probably the fear that I would lose Chanale, or maybe my tremendous will to live. I suppose we can't always be rational. Instinct pushes us to do things that we can't change later. And it was instinct, too, that now made me afraid to remain in the shelter till the front passed our farm. I was afraid the barn might catch fire in the chaos. Avrumeh and I could run out, but what about Mother? Lately, she even had to be helped out of the shelter at night.

I started to persuade Avrumeh that we should all go out to the fields and hide in the straw there. It was July 31, 1944. The wheat had been cut and was still standing in the fields in bundles. The day before, Krynski had told us that he had dug out a large trench not far from the house and would take cover there when the shooting started. His daughter Gienia and his son-in-law from the village would be joining them, and if we wanted, we could come too. But we decided not to go because Gienia and her husband still didn't know that Krynski was harbouring us, and we knew that the Krynskis were afraid of how their son-in-law would react.

Around five o'clock in the morning, Avrumeh looked outside. Not a soul was in sight — only many fires, close together. We decided not to wait for the food we always received around noon, and we left the shelter to sneak into a bundle of wheat near the barn. Around seven o'clock, the shooting became heavier, and it looked like the Germans were just to the other side of us. There was shooting and a tremendous clanging of artillery over our heads.

We were finally outside, but in what condition? We were lying there in the straw, all four of us pressed together. Mother prayed, as she always did, to see us free, and to be able to boil water for herself for tea, since she was always thirsty. Through the fog and smoke, we saw the Soviet soldiers approaching and we heard them yelling. Then they disappeared and the shooting grew even heavier. Our hearts seemed to stop beating for fear that the Germans would come back. We lay there in the wheat the whole day. Near sunset, amid the sound of intense gunfire, we heard rifle shots around us. We felt half dead by then from lying on the ground without moving an inch and without food and water. Avrumeh made a hole in the straw so that he could peek out and see what was going on. He saw a Russian soldier pointing his rifle at us. They were shooting at every bush and into every bundle of wheat to make sure there were no Germans hidden there. My husband screamed, "Russians!" and grabbed Chanale and pushed her out on top of the straw.

The soldier approached and asked, "Who are you? Prisoners or escaped from a camp?" We said, "We are Jews; we are hiding from the Germans." Mother grabbed the soldier's hand and kissed it, saying in Russian, "Thank you for liberating my children." The soldier wiped away a tear. He patted Mother's shoulder and said, "Go to the rear, Babushka. This is the front line. Watch out! Some soldiers might think you are spies. And you don't have to thank me. We will liberate everybody."

Instead of going back to the house, we walked toward the Soviets, passing the advancing army and moving on in the direction where Shieh and Henia were hiding.

As far as we could see, there was a long, long line of Soviet soldiers, marching with their rifles pointed straight out in front of them. I was struck by the extremes of age difference — boys so young that they didn't have beards yet and old men, some bearded, as though all their able-bodied soldiers had been killed. We had already heard rumours that the Soviet Union had lost a tremendous number of people in the war and that many of its cities had been completely destroyed.

We walked on, dragging Mother along, her legs stiff from having lain so long. As we walked, we didn't stop thanking the soldiers, who, in turn, told us to move along behind them. By now it was clear that they couldn't possibly mistake us for spies. Chanale was with us, our clothes were in rags and our pale faces showed that we hadn't seen the sun for a long, long time.

Bittersweet

Freedom was not as sweet as we had dreamed it would be. When we finally walked into Semiatych, although we reunited with Shieh, Henia, Sruleh and Shieleh, we realized how enormous our tragedy was. To get to Avrumeh's parents' house — our own had been a rented apartment and we couldn't go back there — we had to pass the district where most of the Jews had lived before the war. Our feet could hardly carry us, and we wanted to run away. It seemed to me that from every window and door, the ghosts of the people who had once lived there were looking at us with envy, their eyes asking, "How did you survive? Why are you the lucky ones? Why and for what did we have to be burned?" I felt ashamed for being alive.

But the worst thing was to come to my in-laws' house. We had to wait a whole day until the people who were living there were finally forced by the new authorities to allow us to stay in one room — all eight of us in a house of ten rooms, where eleven people from Avrumeh's family had lived for years. I hadn't seen them die, and I couldn't think of them as dead. I had left them all so much alive. In every corner in and around the house, I seemed to see and hear them talking, always asking the same question, "Why?" I again envied all the people who had perished. I was sorry that I wasn't with them, and I thought about my sister-in-law, Chana. How right she had been, that it wasn't worth fighting for a life like this.

We met a few other Jews who had survived. We were all weak and run down. Before the liberation, hope and the tremendous will to survive had given us strength to hold on, but coming to the town and knowing what had happened to all our Jewish people, our community, our strength broke down. We, the younger ones, now had to worry about finding a piece of bread or some potatoes to eat. Mother was in no condition to walk around. Shieh suffered the most. We were liberated. He was alive. But where was his family? And here he had to see me and Henia with our children, whom he had helped to save. His eyes were always red from crying. He lost all his will to live. I knew very well what was going on in his mind and heart. We always had to watch him, and we couldn't leave him alone — we were afraid that he would take his own life.

Among the few Jews we met in Semiatych were Ben Lev and his teenage son. Ben's wife, Maita, had been killed along with my father the night we escaped from the ghetto. Ben had owned a large grain mill before the war. After returning to Semiatych, he got a job there and was allowed to live in a house near the mill. One night, just months after the liberation, his son came home at eleven o'clock to find the door open and his father's bed empty but still warm. With the help of some young Jewish men, he found his father's body not far from the house.

I have no words to describe the pain we all felt then. After having been hidden for almost two years and only just liberated, Ben had been murdered by young Polish men who, instead of fighting their real enemy, the Germans, searched out Jewish survivors to kill in the name of a "pure Polish country."

So, again we lived in fear. I was afraid to send Chanale to school each day because the children called her names. But seeing our lives endangered, Shieh revived once again. And actually, we were lucky to be living in Semiatych because it was near to where the Soviet army was stationed while building up its forces for the attack on Warsaw. Semiatych was full of Soviet soldiers, and they provided a kind of protection.

By the end of December, though, we heard rumours that some of those Polish bandits were planning to finish off the Jews in Semiatych. There was no way we could feel safe now. Afraid even to go to sleep, we tried to invite Soviet soldiers to stay overnight, because they had weapons, but we couldn't always find a willing guest.

One night in the last week of December 1944, two Soviet soldiers were sleeping on the floor of our house, since we had no beds yet. The rest of us were still up and wondering if we would survive this night. Across the road lived two Jewish families with their relative, a young girl from another town who had lost all her immediate family. At midnight we heard an explosion, then a banging on the door. We were afraid to open it. The soldiers stood up and, with their rifles pointed, opened the door. There stood the young Jewish girl, screaming, her face all torn to pieces and streaming with blood. We let her in along with the others from their house. They told us what had happened: As the girl crossed in front of a window, carrying a kerosene lamp and on her way to bed, a hand grenade was thrown in.

That night, I decided that we had to leave Semiatych. I heard that a Jewish community was forming in Białystok, which was just under a hundred kilometres away. Before the war, the city of Białystok had had a large Jewish population — at one point, about fifty thousand Jews lived there. Now, Jewish survivors from all around were moving to the bigger cities to be together. At the first opportunity, Mother, Avrumeh, Chanale and I set out of Semiatych in a Soviet military truck. Again, we hoped that good people — this time, Jewish people — would spare a bit of space for us.

When we got to Białystok, Mother and I walked around the demolished houses to scrounge up whatever we could find for our new household there. Everything we picked up made us feel like crying. We knew the fates of the people who had left behind their belongings in those houses. Eventually we managed to get a house to ourselves and a few pieces of furniture. We tried to make a home again.

Whenever I walked the streets with Chanale, Jewish men would stop us and ask me how I had been able to save her. The only Jews I met in Białystok at that time were young people, most of them single men. It was winter, January and February 1945, and Mother would say, "The sun is shining so brightly, go out with Chanale, you lay enough in the bunker." I always responded, "It's just so hard for me to meet someone who lost a family. I know that when they see Chanale, their hearts cry."

The Soviet army was moving forward on all fronts. We knew that the war was ending and that the Germans were defeated. Although those of us who were left couldn't be really happy with anything, there was a satisfaction in hearing that now Germans were fleeing their homes, leaving everything behind.

On March 2, Mother told me that she felt as though her heart was not beating regularly. When I suggested going to a doctor, she responded, "You think a doctor can replace an old heart? My heart was strong enough to go through all this."

We agreed that Mother would see a doctor the next day. She lay down, and at supper time she felt much better. Later that evening, Avrumeh and Chanale went next door to a Jewish neighbour where young people would gather, and we heard them singing. Mother said to me, "Why don't you go over? You'll hear Chanale sing."

"I'm not in the mood for songs," I said.

"You have your family," she answered, "but you are always sadder than everyone else. Young people have to go on living; you can't stop nature."

I was with her all that evening. We went to bed around midnight. In the morning, I got up early to make a fire in the stove to warm up the room. We were sleeping in the same room, and I was walking on tiptoes so as not to wake Chanale and Mother up, thinking it would do Mother good to sleep in. But it would turn out that she was in a deep sleep forever.

Knowing that this was what she had been praying for — to see us free and to die in her sleep — didn't ease the wound of her death. It was very painful for us to see her die after she had suffered so much, and only seven months after the liberation, before she could see her son and daughter in Montreal or be reunited with her daughter who had been sent to Siberia. This had been her life's dream.

~

One morning at the end of April, we walked out of Białystok, again leaving everything behind, and went south with the streams of other survivors. We waited in a displaced persons camp in Italy for close to three years for our visas to Canada. In May 1948, we landed in Halifax, and then we made our way to Montreal. I was reunited with my brother Hertzke and my sister Chaya, who had come to Canada before the war. Eventually, my youngest sister, Itke, and her husband and children also came to Montreal. Since then, we have enjoyed the freedom of Canada, where so many people live together in peace.

We will never understand why the world allowed that monster and his helpers to come to power and to do what they did to the Jewish people. I am sure that many Poles who belonged to that group of bandits and wanted to make their country "pure Polish" are also enjoying the freedom of Canada. I wonder if they have learned anything about how people of so many different ethnic backgrounds, races and religions can live together peacefully. I really wonder.

Epilogue

In 1959, our Chanale graduated from McGill University in Montreal. Her Jewish name was called out among many others, and she received her degree with distinction for her work, unrelated to her people or her religion. My heart was bursting with joy, but there was also sorrow. Why couldn't Mother have been here to see all this? She had hoped so much to see us happy.

Three weeks later, when I saw Chanale walking down the aisle to be married, I thought, *Is all this a sweet dream*? But when I looked at my brother Shieh, and I saw him wiping his eyes, I knew what he was thinking. I was having the same thoughts: Seventeen years earlier, when it had really mattered, I had tried to assure his wife, Chana, that if we survived, life would be better, but I could not promise her that there was a place where we would be treated equally. Now, reunited with all my sisters and brothers at this joyous occasion of my daughter's wedding, at last I could say, "Yes, Chana, it was worth fighting for our lives; it was worth surviving."

Chana Broder

To the memory of three people that I loved and lost:
my parents, Rachel Kalles Lisogurski and Abraham Lisogurski,
and my dear husband, Menashe Tashie Broder.

What I Remember

I was only a year old when World War II broke out. I was three and a half years old when my parents were forced to move into the ghetto with all the other Jews of the town of Semiatych. My mother's memoir tells the whole story of how we survived and where we hid. As a grown-up, I was never quite sure which of these events and circumstances from the war I actually remembered and which I only recalled my parents recounting. There are, however, two memories from those days that are very vivid in my mind.

The first is of an incident that occurred when we were hiding in Klemens's barn. Somehow, I had slipped through the straw and the slats that formed the floor of our loft and slid down to the barn below. I found myself standing upright and unharmed, among the cows, with the huge, frightening face of a red cow just inches above my own face. I stood there trembling with fear for what seemed like a very long time, until the adults noticed my absence and figured out what had happened. In all that time, I never uttered a sound because it had been drilled into me that I was not allowed to cry or scream no matter what happened.

"What'll happen if I cry?" I had asked my mother during my training sessions, when we were still in our own house.

"Then the Germans will come."

"What'll happen if the Germans come?"

"They'll shoot us."

"What'll happen if they shoot us?"

"Then we'll be dead."

"What'll happen if we're dead?"

On and on, the questions and answers continued until my mother succeeded in training me never to cry.

The second memory, which I am certain I remember, pertains to a day in Krynski's bunker. By that time, I missed my cousin Shieleh, who I used to play with, and I missed seeing the animals in Klemens's barn and the sight of daylight.

It was the day that Pan Krynski came to warn us that there were "boys" from a nationalist group on his property, searching for Jews. Krynski was shaking with fear when he warned us, and he ran off quickly. Perhaps someone in the village had become suspicious and tipped off these thugs, a neighbour who was jealous of the new clothes the Krynskis occasionally wore, or their son's friend, who may have overheard something or been told something in confidence in the tavern. There were many possibilities, but the cause didn't matter anymore. We in the bunker were bracing ourselves for the moment when the trapdoor would be forcibly opened and we would be discovered. I remember that my father took out his pocket watch and buried it in the straw. "For Krynski," he murmured. He extinguished the lantern, and we sat in total darkness, holding hands, silently waiting for death. I will always remember the unique fear I felt during those long moments; it was different from anything I experienced before or after.

~

After liberation, my parents were haunted by the faces of all the Jews who had not returned. A small number of Jews came back from the concentration camps, and they told hair-raising stories of gas chambers, in which thousands of Jews had been murdered every day, and of crematoria in which the bodies had been burned. They told of forced labour, constant hunger, disease, brutal punishments and humiliations. Other Jews came back from hard labour in the Soviet Union. Our family realized that our suffering had been relatively mild.

The Jews who returned found that they were not welcome in their old homes. Some gentiles had seized Jewish properties, and they resented having to return them to their former owners.

I was sent to the local school. I would walk there with another little Jewish girl, and often the gentile children would call us names and sometimes even throw stones at us.

During the war, everyone's energy was focused on survival. Now that we were liberated and the war was almost over, depression set in for many of the adults, caused by the sorrow for all the relatives and friends who had perished and the hatred of the surrounding Polish population. My uncle Shieh was particularly despondent as time went on and he realized that his wife and two daughters had not survived. Even as a six-year-old, I realized that he was terribly nervous and did not have his usual friendly demeanor. Later, as an adult, I learned that my mother and aunt were actually worried that he might commit suicide, as many others did at that time.

What do I remember from those days in Semiatych after we were liberated? I remember that on Yom Kippur, the small number of Jews who had returned gathered for prayers. I remember one man leaning against the wall and sobbing bitterly. Until that day, I had thought that men were physically incapable of weeping because I had never seen a man cry. I remember my cousin Shieleh being sick and delirious with high fever. He was talking nonsense and I was terrified that he was going to die.

Soon, some local thugs tried to force the Jews to leave town. Several Jews were killed and many more were injured. My uncle Shieh was in someone's house when shots were fired into the house through a window. He was wearing a loose leather coat and a bullet went through his coat behind his back, narrowly missing his body.

My parents decided to leave their hometown, and we moved to

Białystok with my grandmother. The others remained in Semiatych. Białystok was a larger city, where a Jewish community of survivors was forming. Survivors from many small but previously vibrant Jewish towns were streaming into Białystok, seeking the comfort of numbers.

My beloved grandmother, Rivka, died in Białystok. Her weak heart finally gave out and she died in her sleep, as I peacefully slept in the same bed. I remember waking up to my mother's screams as she came to see why her mother had not woken up. It was a terrible shock to me because I was very attached to my grandmother. My mother was inconsolable. It was very painful for her to accept the fact that her mother had survived close to two years of running and hiding, of hunger and terror, only to die so soon after our liberation, before the family had reached a safe haven. The only small consolation was that she had died a natural death, in her own bed.

An Actual Childhood

I remember the next period of my life as a time of endless travel and constant confusion. I remember trips on trains and trucks and always walking, carrying bundles and bags. I remember pushing onto crowded railway cars, worrying that I would be crushed in the mayhem or that I would lose my parents forever. I remember my heart beating with fright as we were silently smuggled across borders in the dead of night. I was too young to understand then, but today I know that this was part of the chaos that existed in Europe as the war was coming to an end.

My parents and I left Białystok and went to Lublin, which had become a centre for Jewish refugees, with my auntie Henia, my uncle Sruleh and my cousin Shieleh. I never remembered the exact order of the countries through which we then passed, but now I know that we left Poland at the end of April 1945 and went to Slovakia and then to Hungary. We were in Hungary on May 8, 1945, the day the war in Europe ended. From there we went to the region of Transylvania in Romania, where we stayed for a number of weeks, aiming to get to Constanţa, a Romanian port on the Black Sea. Small boats were sailing from Constanţa into the Mediterranean Sea, trying to go on to Palestine. But most of them were caught by the British navy, who took the passengers to internment camps in Cyprus. The British, who had been ruling in Palestine since the 1920s under a League of Nations mandate, allowed only limited legal Jewish immigration into the territory. Even after the war, the British leaders had other considerations besides the welfare of the homeless, traumatized Jews — such as not antagonizing the Arab population in and around Palestine.

Many Jews were hoping that Britain, one of the enlightened, democratic Allies, would now allow the Jewish refugees into their ancient homeland, if only out of consideration for the terrible suffering that European Jews had undergone at the hands of the Nazis. But this was not to be.

Former soldiers from the Jewish Brigade — Jewish men from Palestine who had volunteered to serve in the British army in order to fight Nazi Germany — now turned their attention to gathering Holocaust survivors and bringing them to Palestine by any means. A few boats succeeded in evading the British patrols. They landed on unmarked beaches, where many local Jews waited for them and whisked them off to various towns and villages before the British forces arrived.

Then the Romanian government closed the route from Constanța so that private ships could not pass through. Our families would have to wait, and no one knew for how long. As a result, we backtracked to Hungary and went to Austria.

As more people joined us, our group of refugees gradually grew larger, and we were handed over from one leader to another. These leaders were representatives from the Jewish Agency, some of whom had been in the brigades as well. Sometimes we stopped for days and sometimes for weeks. In Graz, Austria, we were put up in a beautiful hotel for three days. There was a tiled bathroom in each room, with hot and cold running water. This was a marvel that I had never seen before. But there was very little food because the people in charge had paid for far fewer people than were actually accommodated there. The leaders explained that because the city authorities must not know about the presence of the Jewish refugees, the hotel would be locked and no one allowed out. At night, however, many of the fathers there climbed out the windows and went into the city to buy food for their hungry children.

A special organization had been formed to help resettle the numerous refugees that had been created by the war. This body was called the United Nations Relief and Rehabilitation Administration (UNRRA), and it later became part of the United Nations when that organization was founded in October 1945. My father and my uncle went to register our families with UNRRA, and they received a little money to live on. It soon became evident, however, that UNRRA did not have the authority to send Jews to Palestine.

In the autumn of 1945, we finally crossed the border into Italy, where we would end up remaining for two and a half years. When I think of my childhood memories, I begin with our time in Italy. Everything that came before that was not worthy of being remembered, did not deserve to be preserved in my brain.

We found ourselves in a temporary camp for displaced persons on the outskirts of the beautiful medieval city of Padua. There I celebrated my seventh birthday on October 20, 1945. After a few weeks, we were told that a permanent displaced persons camp was being set up in the city of Cremona and that everyone would have to move there.

My father was weary of being taken and led and told what to do. "I'm an electrician!" he exclaimed. "There's always work for electricians, especially now, after the war, when everything has to be rebuilt and repaired."

"But you can't speak the language," my mother objected.

"Never mind," he told her. "My hands will speak for me."

My father went into the city, and when he returned, he joyfully announced that he had a job. He had not worked at his profession since the beginning of the war, and he was exuberant at the prospect of going back to it now. After a few days, my parents rented a room in the home of an elderly widow, and the three of us moved in. No more handouts for us.

When the camp from Padua was transferred to Cremona, my

auntie Henia and uncle Sruleh moved there as well. Their son, my cousin Shieleh, had moved to a children's home in Selvino that had a rich cultural life, educating the children and eventually hoping to bring them to Palestine, or *Eretz Yisrael*, as we called it, the Land of Israel. Before the war, Shieleh had belonged to a Zionist youth movement, so this institution appealed to him greatly. His parents, though, had to face the dilemma of allowing their one and only son to move away from them after what they had suffered together, but they had agreed to let him go there because he would have regular meals and, above all, he would get an education. I was very sorry to be separated from Shieleh and my aunt and uncle, but soon a whole new world opened up for me.

There was a small Jewish community in Padua, but these Jews did not speak Yiddish. They spoke Italian among themselves and prayed in Hebrew. Strange! The rabbi's wife was the principal of a small school where Jewish children learned to read the Bible in Hebrew and to pray, in addition to the regular studies in Italian. I was enrolled in this school, and in no time at all, I was chattering away in Italian with my new friends. My seven-year-old ears picked up the local accent so perfectly that very soon I could not be distinguished from a native speaker.

In the school, Grades 1 to 3 were taught in the same classroom. Naturally, I was placed in the first grade. After several weeks, I said to my mother, "I know all the answers to the questions that the teacher asks the Grade 2 class."

"Well," my mother replied, "tell your teacher."

When I shyly approached the teacher and gave her this information, she was surprised. She asked me to read something and then to solve some arithmetic problems. She agreed that I knew enough to be in the second grade, so she moved my desk into the middle group. A couple of months later, the process was repeated, and I was promoted to the third grade.

The Italian people were especially kind to the Jewish refugees.

They too had suffered at the hands of the Germans, and they commiserated with the misfortunes that had befallen the Jews. If asked for directions, they would not only explain patiently, but they would even leave their stores unattended and walk with us for blocks just to show us the way. Their kindness was such a contrast to the way that the Polish people had treated Jews that my parents were full of amazement and gratitude.

Those were happy months. My father was working and picking up a little Italian on the job. My mother was delighted to have some money to buy food and prepare it for her family. And I? I finally had the opportunity to be a child, with child-sized problems.

Then an unexpected tragedy occurred. In December 1945, my uncle Sruleh died suddenly of a heart attack. Within days, he was buried in the Jewish cemetery in Milan. We were all thunderstruck. My mother decided that she had to be near her sister to help her through this new disaster, so we moved to the camp in Cremona.

The camp was administered by UNRRA, and food was distributed to each family that wanted to cook for itself. In addition, there was a communal kitchen, where Auntie Henia was one of the cooks. There was a vocational school run by ORT, the Organization for Rehabilitation through Training, and my father was soon employed there to teach the electrician trade to students. I was very proud when I saw him in his navy-blue instructor's coat.

All the cultural life in the camp was organized by *shlichim*, emissaries, from British Mandate Palestine. The language of instruction in our school was Hebrew, so I started over again in Grade 1. This was my third time in Grade 1 — first in Polish, then in Italian, and now in Hebrew. Eventually, I progressed here as well.

There were many children in the Cremona camp, and so many activities. We were taught Israeli songs and dances; there were ballet lessons and Bible lessons outside of the school program; and we celebrated all the Jewish holidays. Sometimes adults put on plays, and other times the children did, all by ourselves. I discovered that I had quite a talent for acting, and this brought me praise and satisfaction.

Although we spoke Hebrew in school among ourselves, when we played, the common language was Yiddish. I was amazed to hear the variety of Yiddish dialects and accents, yet we children managed to understand each other, even though we often had arguments about the proper pronunciation of this or that word. The most unfortunate children were those who did not know any Yiddish when they arrived. They had to learn it, along with Hebrew, in order not to be ostracized by the other children in the camp.

During this time, my parents made contact with their relatives in North America. My father had two aunts and two uncles in the United States, and my mother's sister Chaya and her brother Hertzke had immigrated to Canada before the war. All these relatives applied for permission to bring us over. My father also received a letter from an uncle in Wales who had left Poland before my father was born. My father had forgotten about his existence, although he had heard about him from his father.

There was a constant debate among the inhabitants of the camp as to whether it was preferable to go to Palestine or to America. One side argued that America was still a *goyishe* (non-Jewish) land, that Jews were still strangers there and there was no guarantee that what had happened in Germany could not happen one day in America. The Jews needed a land of their own. The other side countered that the world had not yet agreed to give Palestine to the Jews, and that even if this decision was made, the Arabs in Palestine would start a war and wipe them all out.

My mother was inclined to go live in a Jewish state, if such a state was established. But my father convinced her that a Jewish state in Palestine meant inevitable war with the Arabs, and he personally could not bear to go through another war. He had lost his whole family in the war. He was no longer the joking, singing young man he had been; very often he was depressed. My mother could not oppose him. She conceded that we would go to the United States or Canada, whichever would be the first to let us in.

My auntie Henia had decided to go to Canada, which caused a problem for my cousin Shieleh. The director of the children's home in Selvino was urging him to go to *Eretz Yisrael* and fulfill the Zionist dream. He was enthusiastic about going to live in Palestine, but a lot of pressure was placed on him to go to Canada with his widowed mother. He even received a letter from our uncle in Montreal, trying to convince him that it was his duty to take care of his mother and not to separate from her. It was a very difficult decision for a boy of fifteen to make. Finally, he chose duty over desire and left Selvino to come be with us in Cremona.

One day in the early spring of 1948, we were summoned by the Canadian embassy in Rome to discuss our upcoming immigration. Not just my parents and I, but Henia and Shieleh too. Such excitement! A visit to Rome! Since we children spoke Italian better than the adults, we were the interpreters for our families.

After the official business was taken care of, we used this occasion to visit the Vatican, which the adults had heard about even in Poland. The elevator to the top of St. Peter's Basilica was out of order, so Shieleh and I climbed the hundreds of stairs together to see the magnificent view. When we came back down, our legs were shaking from the effort. Then we all gaped at the beauty of the Sistine Chapel, with Michelangelo's gloriously painted ceiling.

In April 1948, we packed our meagre belongings, and we were on our way again. We crossed the ocean on a large Polish ship, the *Sobieski*. Here were more wonders that I had never experienced — decks with staircases to be explored and dining rooms where meals were served to us by waiters. Except for a little seasickness, it was a wonderful week. As we approached Halifax, we all hoped we would find a permanent home in Canada.

New Lands

On May 2, 1948, we took the train from Halifax to Montreal — me, my mother and father, my aunt and my cousin. All I remember of our arrival in Montreal is a lot of people at Windsor Station, all of them wearing hats. I thought that they had all come to meet us.

On May 14, 1948, the State of Israel was declared. In later years, I always marvelled at the fact that I had no recollection of this event. The excitement of arriving in our new home and the thousands of new perceptions evidently overshadowed the memory of this historic milestone, which must have been very significant in the lives of my family.

My parents and I went to live with my mother's brother Hertzke, his wife, Tzirl, and their two children, Eudice, who was thirteen, and Emmanuel, who was four. Henia and Shieleh moved in with Henia's twin sister, my auntie Chaya, her husband, Shloimeh (Sam), and my cousin Marcia, who was also four years old. It was very exciting to discover these new relatives.

There was a shortage of houses in Montreal after the war that had increased with the influx of new immigrants, so it took us several months to find an apartment to rent. Eventually, we moved into a one-bedroom apartment on Park Avenue, a busy commercial street, in a building owned by my mother's Uncle Idl, who was married to Auntie Leicheh. They lived in the building and so did their daughter

Fay and her family. Auntie Manya and her daughter Annie lived nearby. All these people enveloped us in a warm blanket of caring and support.

I was sent to a private Jewish day school, the Jewish People's School, also known as the Folks Shule. I was afraid that I would start in Grade 1 again, for the fourth time, but the principal, Shloime Wiseman, said that I belonged in Grade 4 since I was nine and a half years old.

On the first day of school, the teacher asked me whether I could read English. I'd had a few months of private English lessons as soon as our visa for Canada had come through, so I answered that I could read a little. The teacher then asked me to read aloud the beginning of the story that the class was studying in the reader. "The Oogly Doockling..." I began, and the whole class burst out laughing. I never forgot that laughter.

Very soon it was summer vacation, and I was sent to a summer camp run by the Jewish community. I spent three wonderful weeks there, and after those three weeks, I came back speaking English fluently. Although my vocabulary was not very extensive, I had picked up the accent and the idioms of the other children. During the course of the next year, I progressed by leaps and bounds. Like a sponge, I absorbed the new language, the subjects taught in school and the new rules of socializing with my peers. By the end of that year, I was one of the top students in my class. Nobody laughed at me anymore. I was not in the most popular clique in the class, but I had several good friends. One curious price of learning English was that I forgot Italian almost completely. It was incomprehensible to my parents, and indeed to me, how someone who had spoken a language like a native could lose it entirely.

During our second summer in Canada, I went to Unzer Camp, a camp for Jewish children affiliated with the Labour Zionist Movement of Montreal. We sang Hebrew and Yiddish songs and learned Israeli folk dances in addition to the sports, swimming and arts and crafts activities that were typical of any Canadian summer camp. I made new friends there.

In the fall, I joined Habonim, a Labour Zionist youth movement, where I was taught to identify with the new Jewish homeland of Israel and to strive to live there. My best childhood memories are from my days in Habonim and its summer camp, Camp Kvutza. I loved singing Hebrew songs and dancing Israeli dances. I even loved the serious ideological discussions about socialist Zionism. And of course, I revelled in the camaraderie, in the feeling of identity and belonging.

The Folks Shule did not have a high school at that time — that would come later, during the 1970s — so I went to Baron Byng High School, where the students were almost exclusively Jewish. Throughout my four years of high school, I also attended Jewish classes at the Folks Shule twice a week after school and on Sunday mornings. My marks were always at the top of the class in both schools.

When I was near the end of Grade 10, I was asked to the senior prom by a boy named Normie. This was the most exciting thing that could have happened to me. Normie was the editor of the school magazine, and he had run for president of the Students' Council and had lost by only a small margin. In short, he was a very popular, intelligent guy and he had asked me to his senior prom!

What to wear? I didn't own anything that would be suitable for such an occasion, so Annie Dickstein, who was engaged to my cousin Shieleh (now called Sidney), took me to a clothing factory, where I bought an aqua-coloured strapless semi-formal dress. I was afraid that my mother would think it was too grown-up, but she gave her approval. I realized later that my mother must have derived a great deal of vicarious pleasure from this whole adventure.

I had a marvellous time at the senior prom. Afterwards, we went to a nightclub and then to a popular restaurant for breakfast. I fell head-over-heels in love with Normie and we continued to date for a year, until my senior prom. By that time, things had turned sour and I did not like the way he was treating me. I was sure he would end it any day, so I preserved my pride by breaking up with him, even though it broke my heart.

~

My parents worked very hard to establish themselves in this new land. They had come from Europe with two suitcases of worn-out clothes and those were the sum total of their assets. My father got a job with an electrical contractor, an owner of a very small business. My mother went to work in a factory that manufactured ladies' coats. She was a finisher, sewing by hand those parts of the coat that could not be done on a machine, and she was paid by the piece. That meant that the more she worked, the more she earned. My aunt Henia worked in the same place at the same job. The two of them and another woman who had recently come from Czechoslovakia worked incessantly, not even taking lunch breaks. They ate their thick sandwiches at their workstations, not willing to sacrifice the extra time it would take to go to the workers' lunchroom.

My parents did not go to restaurants, they did not go away on vacations, and they bought only the clothes that were absolutely necessary. They spent no money on luxuries. Pretty soon, through hard labour and great thrift, they were able to buy a modest house. This was extremely significant to them after the years of wandering and homelessness during the war.

When I finished high school, I wanted to go to Israel to participate in the Habonim Workshop program, a special year of work and study, but my parents would not hear of it. My mother was especially adamant. "You are our only child. I have given birth to you not once but ten times. I don't want you to move away to Israel. You will go there now for a year, but they will influence you to go live there for good. Oh, no, you are too young to make such decisions. You know that our greatest dream is for you to go to university and learn a profession. When you're grown up, if you still want to live in Israel, we won't be able to stop you."

My mother was hoping that by the time I was grown up, I would forget my idealistic nonsense and would marry a nice Jewish boy and settle down to raise a family. In her heart, however, she always feared that one day Israel might lure her only child away from her.

I realized that this was an argument I could never win, so I gave in. I went to McGill University and got a bachelor's degree in mathematics and biology. I was no longer an outstanding student, but my grades were quite respectable. I was thinking of going on to do a master's degree in genetics so that I could have a career in research and teaching at the university level.

That was before I got involved with Menashe Broder, known to all his friends as Tashie. I had known Tashie casually for many years. He had gone to the Folks Shule and was only a year ahead of me. He also was a member of Habonim, but he attended activities irregularly. I thought of Tashie, when I thought of him at all, as wild, undisciplined and unreliable.

My best friend, Machle, had a brother, Bernie, who was much older. When Machle and I were seventeen, Bernie got married, and I was invited to Bernie's wedding because I was considered a member of their family. According to custom at that time, I was entitled, as a single guest, to invite a partner for the dancing that would follow the chuppah and the meal. Bernie, who had also belonged to Habonim when he was younger, had invited all the young people of Habonim to come for the dancing, which is how Tashie happened to be there. And as it turned out, the boy I had invited was sick that night and didn't show up at all. Tashie moved right in, asking me to dance again and again. It was obvious that he was trying to charm me, and I found it very flattering. At the end of the evening, he asked if he could take me home and I agreed. We always considered that night, November 6, 1955, as the anniversary of the beginning of our romance.

Tashie was tall, very thin, with dark hair and brown eyes and a long nose. He did not fit my ideal image of a handsome boy, but I was attracted by his wiry energy and the way he walked with his head forward, as if testing the air before he went into it. Tashie was intelligent, athletic and well-liked. Above all, he made me feel special. He began to hang around the places that I frequented and told me quite bluntly that he was there because of me. He would wait for hours through Habonim meetings that bored him just for the pleasure of driving me home in his father's car. I felt flattered by his attentions and by the silly little presents he bought me.

Most of all, I was impressed by the fact that he bared his soul to me. He spoke to me about his problems with his parents, his difficulties at university, his doubts about the future. The few boys I had dated previously had never exposed their insecurities; they had always seemed so confident, so self-assured. I was touched by Tashie's vulnerability. Before long, I knew that I loved him dearly, just as he loved me.

A few years later, when we began to discuss marriage, we considered the possibility of moving to Israel. We dismissed it, however, because we were too busy with personal plans of careers and marriage to be concerned with idealism. I gave up my plan of going into research in genetics because it meant that I would not be able to earn money for a long time. Instead, I was going to get a teacher's diploma, which would take only one year, so that I could work and support the two of us while Tashie went to study law. We were married on June 21, 1959, three weeks after we each received a bachelor's degree.

Tashie and I had a beautiful wedding, not ostentatious, but in good taste. I wore a full-length gown of organza trimmed with lace, with a billowing skirt and several crinolines underneath. My mother, for the first time in her life, also wore a full-length gown. Hers was a pale blue satin with embroidered borders. The other women and girls in the wedding party wore various shades of blue and turquoise, and the men wore white dinner jackets. The sumptuous, generous meal was followed by a lavish sweet table. There was a band for ballroom dancing and an accordionist for folk dancing whenever the band took a break. Only years later did I appreciate what a great achievement it had been for my parents, only eleven years in Canada, to have hosted such a reception. Tashie's parents, Sam and Ellen, had offered to share the expenses, but my parents had refused. They were so proud that they could afford to give their one and only daughter the kind of wedding they had not been able to imagine when they first arrived in Canada.

Tashie and I had worked part-time during our last years in university and had saved our money for a honeymoon in Israel. Tashie was able to contribute most of this money because he'd had only a few courses to finish in the last semester and he worked full-time as a substitute teacher. Our parents thought that the money we'd saved could be put to better use toward a house or a car, but we were determined to go visit Israel, the land we had learned about and dreamt about, while we were still free of responsibilities and obligations. If necessary, we were prepared to add some of our wedding-gift money to make this trip of a lifetime.

The entire honeymoon was like a fairy tale for us — a leisurely journey by ship across the Atlantic, with stops in London and Paris, followed by a shorter Mediterranean voyage culminating in the Promised Land itself. It was love at first sight. The vitality and vibrancy of Israel, which had been an independent state for only eleven years, awoke in both of us all the old ideals and emotions. Here was the realization of the ancient dream, the answer to the prayers of our ancestors for two thousand years, the fulfillment of the early Zionists' vision. Our hearts longed to be a part of it, to share in this exciting enterprise of the return of the Jewish people to our ancient land, to be pioneers. But our heads were busy with plans for university, careers in law and in teaching and a desire to remain with our family and friends. For me, especially, the idea of leaving my parents seemed impossible.

I cried as we left Israel, and the beautiful dream faded. Who knew when I would be back? We returned to Canada and became busy with our new lives, individually and together. These were demanding times, filled with studies and work, adjusting to living together and getting by on meagre financial means.

In 1963, after we had been married for four years, our first daughter, Pnina, was born. By this time, Tashie had graduated from law school and was just beginning to set up a private practice. I had taught for three years and was now going to continue teaching on a half-day basis while my mother looked after the baby. My mother had continued working in the factory even though, financially, there was no need for her to work so hard. When I got married and moved out of the house, I had begged my mother to stop working. "When you have a baby, I'll stop working and help you," my mother had said. And so she did.

In 1966, my uncle Shieh died of a heart attack. He was survived by his second wife, Hela, and their son, Ephraim (Freddy). The following year, our son was born. We named him Sheldon David and called him Shelly, though he later came to be known as David, which he preferred. (He insisted that we call him David because Shelly, he said, was a girl's name.) Our financial situation was much better then, so I was able to employ a woman to take care of him while I continued teaching part-time, and my mother finally had the luxury of being a full-time homemaker.

Meanwhile, Tashie was becoming more and more active in the Zionist organizations in Montreal and held various elected posts. In his official capacities, he took several trips to Israel and was even sent as a delegate to the prestigious World Zionist Congress, where representatives from the Jewish world congregated.

Tashie began to speak about wanting to move to Israel. All his Zionist activities made no sense, he said, unless he was willing to make aliyah, to ascend to Israel. Furthermore, his sister Gitty and her husband, Gabe, had moved to Israel with their daughter, Davida, three years earlier, and they were doing well. They provided both an example and a potential source of help and support.

During the Christmas-New Year vacation of 1967–1968, I left the children with my parents and joined Tashie on a trip to Israel. It was six months after Israel's victory in the Six-Day War and the mood in the country was euphoric. There were new territories and sites to visit: the Western Wall and Old Jerusalem, which had been under Jordanian rule during our first visit; Bethlehem and Hebron; and the Golan Heights in the north. The old magic worked its spell again. Tashie declared that he wanted to move to Israel. Gitty and Gabe, with whom we stayed, urged Tashie and me to come join them.

I longed to say, "Yes, let's do it!" But how could I leave my parents and move so far away? My mother's words echoed in my mind: "I gave birth to you not once, but ten times." Only now that I was older and a mother myself could I begin to understand how their love for me had motivated the risks my parents had taken and the sacrifices they had made. And the grandchildren! They were the pride and joy of my parents' lives. How could I take them away? Did my parents deserve such treatment when they were always ready to help us, financially and in every other way? It was a terrible dilemma.

When we came back from Israel, we discussed the problem. "How can you sit here in Canada and miss the opportunity to be a part of the greatest event that has happened to the Jewish people in two thousand years?" Tashie argued. "Don't you want our children to grow up as proud Jews, not taking second place to anyone?"

"Of course I do. But I can't do this to my parents — you don't understand. Our relationship is not the same as that of other children and their parents. My parents risked their lives every day in order to save me. Their chances of survival would have been much greater without me. But they didn't abandon me or leave me with gentiles, as many other parents did at that time. Your parents have other children, other grandchildren. My parents have only us."

Finally, Tashie came up with the winning argument: "Your first duty is to your children, not to your parents. Just as your parents did what they thought was best for you and not for their parents, so you must do what you think is best for your children. If you think they should grow up in Israel, then it's clear what your decision must be."

I had no answer for that. Besides, I realized that I could not continue to oppose him. His desire to live in Israel was so strong that I would have no peace until I agreed.

The hardest part was telling my parents. My mother was sad but understanding. Having her children and grandchildren so far away would be very difficult for her, but she had always feared this would happen. She could even condone the decision to a certain extent. She admitted to me that if she were younger, and if she had not lived through the terrible experiences of World War II, she too would want to live in Israel.

My father, however, was a different story. Although he was a Zionist — and as his financial situation had improved, he began to donate money to Israel — the war and the loss of his entire family had made him bitter and cynical, and material comforts were very important to him. He did not believe in any ideals except making life safe and more pleasant for himself and for those he loved.

He and my mother had visited Israel on an organized tour and were very impressed with the achievements of the young country. It was wonderful, he thought, to have a homeland for the Jews at last, a refuge for the homeless, a symbol for every Jew to be proud of — just not as an actual home for him and his own, thank you. He could not fathom how anyone could leave the affluence of a middle-class life in Montreal to go chasing ideological rainbows in a new, undeveloped country that was always either at war or on the brink of war. The very idea perplexed and angered him. That we would just pick up and move to the other side of the globe? This was the thanks he got for everything he had done for me and Tashie and our children? He would no longer be able to drive Pnina home from school or take Shelly to his friend Benny's delicatessen to show off the child's cleverness to his buddies. He wouldn't be able to watch his grandchildren grow and develop. It simply wasn't fair!

When Tashie and I made the decision to move to Israel, we planned to do it three years later, in the summer of 1971. Tashie estimated that it would take us that long to save enough money for the move because houses in Israel were very expensive. However, in the spring of 1970, Tashie's father was diagnosed with a malignant brain tumor.

It was inconceivable that Sam Broder, whom everyone loved, should be stricken with this terrible disease. The whole family was to undergo ten months of horror. Surgeons were able to remove the tumor, but the operation left Sam severely impaired, no longer able to walk and unable to perform the simplest tasks. His mind was confused but he understood that he was in great trouble and, as a result, he cried a lot. It was a pitiful sight for me to see my jovial father-in-law, who had always had a smile and a joke for everyone, in this state.

Before Sam got sick, his daughter Rivka, Tashie's younger sister, had been planning to get married at the end of that August. Eventually, my mother-in-law decided to go ahead with the wedding, and although it was a beautiful occasion, it was very sad. Everything was overshadowed, at least for the family, by Sam's condition.

Tashie knew that his father was dying, and he realized that he could not leave his mother alone in Montreal at this time. His older brother, Gaby, lived in Winnipeg; his sister Gitty lived in Israel; Rivka and her new husband, Billy, were moving to Hamilton. Only Tashie was left in Montreal and he knew that he could not leave just yet. He was still determined to move to Israel but decided to postpone our plan by a year.

Both Tashie and I knew that if we were going to make the big move, it had to be while the children were still small. If we waited until they reached their teens, our problems of adjusting to the new environment would only be multiplied. So that December, Tashie and I went on a brief trip to Israel to buy a place to live, settling on a condominium that had not yet been built in Ramat Aviv, on the outskirts of Tel Aviv.

Sam Broder died the following March, in 1971, after nearly a year of suffering for him and for his family. He was not quite seventy-one years old.

Tashie and I and our two children left for Israel the following year, when the school year ended. After four years of anticipation and dread, of saving money and studying Hebrew, the day of departure finally drew near. Then there was a mad flurry of shopping and packing and endless goodbye parties.

There was a terribly tearful scene at the airport when I had to say goodbye to my parents. I boarded the plane with a swollen face and red eyes. Eventually, I calmed down and began to concern myself with the comfort of my children, eight-year-old Pnina and five-year-old Shelly.

Tashie squeezed my hand. The great adventure had begun!

Adjustments and Surprises

In August 1972, we arrived in Tel Aviv and moved into Beit Brodetsky, an absorption centre for new immigrants. We lived there for eight months until we moved into our own condominium apartment. In the absorption centre, we had two rooms, a small kitchenette and a bathroom. It was a little cramped after our large house in Montreal, but not too uncomfortable.

Beit Brodetsky had a cafeteria where we could have a hot meal at a very reasonable price, a lounge and a television room where we could get to know other residents, a telephone for messages that were left for us and a payphone that we could use. In addition, on the premises was an *ulpan*, a school for adults to learn Hebrew. However, since the *ulpan* in Beit Brodetsky taught only beginning and intermediate levels, and Tashie and I were both tested and deemed to be at the advanced level, we had to take our classes in another *ulpan* in downtown Tel Aviv, some distance away.

A few weeks after our arrival, school began and the whole family went off to study. Pnina entered Grade 4 of the local elementary school, Shelly started kindergarten and Tashie and I went to *ulpan*. We had a lot of concerns around our children adjusting to their new schools and the new language, but we all gradually adapted to life in Israel.

Tashie studied for his exams to requalify as an attorney in Israel and be accepted to the Israeli Bar. He passed the exams on the first try! Then he applied himself to the task of finding a job. After several weeks of phone calls and interviews, he was accepted by the legal department of Israel Aircraft Industries.

It all turned out to be much easier than I had imagined during sleepless nights in Montreal. I had heard so many awful stories of North Americans who had moved to Israel and then gone back to North America because they could not find work in their fields, or could not master the Hebrew language, or could not stand the Middle Eastern bureaucracy or the rudeness of the people, or the dirt in the streets.... There was no doubt about it — life in Israel was different from life in North America and some people could not adapt to it.

Some immigrants also suffered from loneliness, having no family or friends in Israel. We were fortunate because we had a fairly large support system. First of all, as I mentioned, there were Gitty and Gabe, who had come to Israel with their little girl, Davida, eight years earlier. They invited us for dinner every Friday night while we were in the absorption centre, and after we moved into our own apartment, we alternated houses each week. These weekly get-togethers in a warm family atmosphere were very valuable to Tashie and the children and me. It gave us a chance to discuss the week's events, to voice our frustrations and to receive advice on how to cope with the many novel and puzzling experiences we were having in our new environment. Davida, who was now a teenager, had grown up in Israel without any grandparents, uncles, aunts or cousins, and she in particular appreciated being surrounded by family.

I also had more distant relatives in Israel, cousins of my parents who had arrived directly from Europe after World War II, at the time that my parents had gone to Canada. They and their children, who had been born in Israel, provided us with a large extended family. We were particularly close to my second cousin, Shoshana, and her husband, Igal, who had spent several years in Montreal. In addition, there were friends who had also come from Montreal. We especially enjoyed visiting friends who lived on kibbutzim. The communal kibbutz was a way of life so different from anything that we had experienced that it was an adventure to visit them. Our children loved picking oranges right off the trees, or jumping in huge piles of cotton seeds or playing with the animals in the petting zoo, activities that were not part of the repertoire of their city life. They even thought that eating in the communal dining room was fun, even though the food was not quite as tasty as their mother's cuisine.

Tashie believed that we had succeeded in our absorption into Israeli life because we came well-prepared and without any illusions. We had visited Israel several times, and we knew what we could expect from life in Israel. We also spoke Hebrew fairly well, and we had saved sufficient money to tide us over a year or more of unemployment, if necessary.

I accepted all these reasons for our successful adaptation to Israeli life, but I also gave credit to an additional factor — luck. Tashie was brilliant, of course, and charming and diligent. But surely luck was also involved in Tashie's getting the position that he did. There had been 130 applicants for the job, and my Tashie was chosen! Secretly, I believed that my lucky stars were at work again, but I never said this in front of Tashie.

In the spring of 1973, we moved into our new apartment. We bought new furniture and unpacked the lift we had sent from Montreal. There was a lot of work and a lot of excitement. The children were now within walking distance of their schools and this made them doubly happy because they no longer had to ride the bus twice a day and could go play in the schoolyard in the afternoons.

My parents arrived for their first visit a few weeks later, just before Passover. The weekly letters my mother and I had exchanged during the previous eight months had kept each of our families informed of the other's activities and served as a significant bond in our relationship, and my father's anger had cooled a little.

The visit was a great success and my parents helped us settle into the new apartment. My mother sewed curtains and advised me where to put various pieces of furniture. My father hung the chandelier, built shelves and did small repairs. He bought the children new bicycles. We all went shopping together and visited relatives.

On the night of the seder, the ritual feast that inaugurates the seven days of Passover in Israel, we all went to the home of Gitty and Gabe. We read from the Haggadah, as we had done every year, and shared a festive and sumptuous dinner to which my mother and I had also contributed. My parents saw that their children were surrounded by loving family and good friends.

All in all, my parents went home with the feeling that their children had not done so badly. We were living in a nice apartment in a good neighbourhood. Tashie had a good job, and in the fall, I would begin teaching English in a high school in Tel Aviv. The children looked happy and healthy and were chattering away in Hebrew, even to each other. My father promised that they would come again in winter, for Chanukah. The following year, the children and I would spend the summer holidays in Montreal and Tashie would join us for his vacation.

Over the years, Tashie and I tried to convince my parents to move to Israel, but in this we were not successful. My mother might have agreed, but my father would not hear of it. "You can't expect that just because you chose to move to Israel, we will come running after you," he said during one particularly heated discussion on the subject. "After all, it was you who left us, not the other way around!" I realized then that my father still felt that he had been rejected and abandoned. There was a lot of bitterness left.

There were times when I missed my parents terribly, especially at holidays, birthdays or graduations. But I began to accept the possibility that my parents might never immigrate to Israel. I concluded that this was part of the price I had to pay for my own aliyah. My parents would either come to live in Israel as a result of their own decision, or not at all. There was nothing more I could do about it, except to ensure that the relationship between us remained close and warm by keeping the lines of communication open.

And so it went — visits back and forth, letters and occasional phone calls. We made sure that the link was not broken, that we did not lose touch and grow apart. We were very much a part of each other's lives.

~

During my mother's first visit to Israel, she confided to me that she had written a book. I was astonished.

"What? When? In what language?" I asked.

My mother explained that she had wanted to improve her English, especially reading and writing. She had never had any formal schooling in English; everything she knew had been picked up by listening and speaking. My aunt Itke had a neighbour named Rose Salzman who was a schoolteacher, and they arranged for my mother to come to her for English lessons. When my mother told Rose that she was interested in learning to write proper English, she said, "Write something and we will correct it together."

"What shall I write?" my mother asked.

"Why don't you write about your experiences during the war?"

So, in 1967, my mother began to write the story of our survival. She wrote a section a week and her teacher corrected the spelling, grammar and so forth. When she finished her story, my mother took typing lessons because she wanted to type up her manuscript. All this time, she told no one about her project — not my father, not her sisters or her brothers, and not me. Finally, when she was finished typing it, she brought the manuscript to Israel and divulged it to me.

I was flabbergasted. That she had invested so much time and effort without sharing her secret with anyone in the family seemed amazing to me. When I had finished reading it, crying, I did not know what else to do with it. I knew that it would not be published commercially.

By that time, the world was surfeited with books about the Holocaust. Also, although subjectively it was very special to me because it was our story, I nevertheless knew that, objectively, there was nothing unique about it to appeal to a publisher or to the public. Some years later, after the first shock abated, there would be a great resurgence of interest and research into the accounts of survivors, but at that time it was just one more Holocaust story like so many others. The world was weary of Holocaust stories. What to do with this treasure?

I phoned the various organizations that dealt with the memory of the Holocaust in Israel, but none of them were interested in publishing another Holocaust story, and certainly not in English. Perhaps our story was not dramatic enough for some people. We had always felt like second-class survivors — we had not slaved in a concentration camp, we had not smelled the odour of the crematoria smoke, we had not been forced on a death march. We had "only" hidden like mice in holes for twenty months, suffered hunger and cold, feared for our lives every day and night.

My son, David, suggested we publish my mother's book privately. I realized then how right he was. Here was an invaluable document, an authentic voice bearing witness to the events of those years at a time when other voices were being raised to deny those events. It was then that I started the process that finally led to the first publication of my mother's book in 1987.

First, I hired someone to edit the manuscript. It was written the way that my mother spoke, so I asked the editor, Toby Mostysser, not to make it too perfect. I wanted to hear my mother's voice come through. Sima Gandelman typed up the edited draft. I titled the book *Out of the Depths* and had it published in Montreal, where my uncle Hertzke and cousin Emmanuel supervised the process. I sent copies to all the libraries I could think of and all the Holocaust organizations that had not wanted to publish the book. My mother wanted to charge a minimal price in order to recover the expenses, but I gave it away for free to anyone who wanted to read it. I wanted the world to know our story. When my children grew up, I also gave it to them to read. My whole family used the book as a reference for things we had forgotten or never knew.

When I reread the manuscript recently, several things became clear to me. Firstly, I understood to what a great extent our survival had depended on luck. Which door we knocked on, which road we took or failed to take, whom we met or missed meeting — these were the factors that determined our survival. Those who made the wrong choices are not here to tell their tale. I was fortunate enough to have won the most fateful lottery of my life, and that was also my prize — life.

I was always aware of the fact that I survived to a large measure because of my parents' love for me. What I now learned was that the great love my parents bore for me gave them more courage and spurred them on to greater efforts, and that love was thus also instrumental in their survival. In our case, unlike in so many others, love triumphed over death.

The Yom Kippur War

Yom Kippur is considered the holiest day in the Jewish calendar. This day occurs ten days after Rosh Hashanah, the Jewish New Year. Observant Jews spend the day fasting and praying in synagogue, believing that on this day God seals the fate of all humankind for the coming year — who will live and who will die, who will be healthy and who will be ill, who will prosper and who will be poor and so on.

On our first Yom Kippur in Israel, Tashie and I were amazed to see that there was no traffic in the streets and that the big highway near our house was silent. Even non-observant Jews parked their cars for twenty-four hours out of respect for the holiness of the day. If you wanted to visit someone who lived far away, you planned to stay there overnight, till the holiday ended, or you walked. The hush that was created by the absence of motors was an extraordinary thing, like a feeling of awe in the air. There were no radio or television broadcasts on Yom Kippur, and all places of business and entertainment, not just restaurants, were closed. We realized that Yom Kippur in Israel was definitely a unique phenomenon.

On Friday, October 5, 1973, on the eve of our second Yom Kippur in Israel, Tashie and I took our children for a walk around the neighbourhood. We no longer went to synagogue because we were not believers. In Montreal, we had gone to synagogue on Rosh Hashanah and on Yom Kippur out of a need to identify with Jewish people the world over and a desire to convey this identification to our children. But here in Israel, in our communities, there was no problem of connecting to Judaism — the vast majority of people were Jewish, and you could never forget it for a moment.

Although I did not attend synagogue, I still fasted every Yom Kippur. If asked why, I would probably say that it was because I had fasted every year since I was twelve years old; it also had something to do with a feeling of belonging to the whole Jewish nation and with the continuation of a historical tradition that stretched back more than two thousand years. These were the same reasons I kept a kosher kitchen, more or less, although I ate non-kosher food outside my own home. Not all reasons for our actions are rational.

On that Yom Kippur eve, we ate our dinner at 4:15 p.m. because the fast was to begin at 5:00, at sundown. Then I washed the dishes and changed my clothes, and the whole family set out for a walk.

The sight that we encountered was astounding. Droves of people were out in the streets, not on the sidewalks, but on the roads, most of them dressed in holiday finery. Older children and teenagers congregated in groups; younger children took advantage of the absence of cars to ride their bicycles on the road; young parents pushed baby carriages and strollers. It seemed like all the residents of the neighbourhood were in the streets.

When we approached the local synagogue, it was almost impossible to pass through the throng of people. It was as if the crowd, though not attending the services themselves, still drew a measure of holiness from the synagogue.

We met neighbours from our building and stopped to chat for a while. From time to time, snatches of singing could be heard from the synagogue above the din of the crowd.

We continued walking for a long time, until our feet ached. Every now and then, the children would greet a friend from school or Tashie and I would nod to a neighbour. "G'mar chatima tova," we would say. "May you be sealed for a good year."

When we came back home, we met several of our neighbours. The building was a new one, less than a year old, so we had all moved in within the previous few months and there was a warm feeling of camaraderie among us. "What I am really looking forward to," one of the neighbours said, "is sleeping in tomorrow morning, without the sound of traffic that wakes me every Saturday."

Little did any of us know what the next day would bring.

Around seven the next morning, Tashie and I were awakened by the sound of airplanes overhead. "Planes on Yom Kippur?" Tashie said drowsily. "Must be a raid on Syria. The religious politicians will raise hell about why it had to be done on this particular day." We both went back to sleep.

At 2:30 in the afternoon, Gitty phoned. "Have you heard? There's a war! Put on your radio."

"What radio? There's no radio on Yom Kippur," I answered.

"There is now!" my sister-in-law said. "This is an emergency."

Tashie turned on the radio.

"The spokesman for the Israel Defense Forces is announcing that shortly before two o'clock this afternoon, Egyptian forces crossed the Suez Canal and are now attacking our positions in the south," we heard. "Syrian forces are also attacking our positions in the north. The reserve army is being called up. Please stay tuned for the reserve codes and for further announcements." The announcer kept repeating the same message over and over again.

Tashie and I dressed quickly and rushed over to the apartment where his mother, Ellen, lived since moving to Israel the previous year. Ellen was an observant woman. She had come back from synagogue a short while before and was unaware of the catastrophe. I expected my mother-in-law to be hysterical, but in fact, this woman, who made a crisis out of any little mishap, was in total control of herself.

When we arrived at my house, I said, "The first thing we are all going to do is have a cup of tea and a piece of bread. This is no time for fasting."

Surprisingly, Ellen did not argue.

At four o'clock in the afternoon, we heard a siren. It had a terrible, frightening sound that rose and fell, assaulting the ear; it seemed to last forever. I was totally disoriented. Tashie, remaining calm at least outwardly, told us that it meant we had to go down to the shelter.

By law, every building of recent vintage had a bomb shelter in the basement. Every single-family home had a specially reinforced room, which might have other uses but also served as a shelter in time of emergency. In the older areas, where individual homes didn't have shelters, there were public shelters. There were also communal shelters in parks, shopping malls, movie theatres and other public places.

Once in the shelter, my initial feeling of panic gradually faded — the atmosphere was more like that of a social gathering than of a crisis. The children all thought it was an occasion for a good time and they romped around noisily.

After about twenty minutes, the all-clear signal was sounded. It was a long, smooth sound, unlike the rising and falling of the alarm. All the residents went back to their apartments. The older children were mobilized to sweep out the shelter; the younger ones wanted to help or at least to watch.

We continued to listen to the news on the radio and we watched it on television. When we were finally able to call my parents from a friend's house (our new building still did not have telephone lines), my father said, "Why don't you come home?"

"This is our home now," I replied, "and we will stay here."

There are only four days between Yom Kippur and the festival of Sukkot. The schools were always closed for a week's vacation on Sukkot, but under the circumstances, with many male teachers and principals mobilized in the army, it had been decided to close the schools for these additional four days. That would give everyone a chance to make arrangements for the classes whose teachers were absent. The decision meant that I would not be teaching for the next twelve days.

By the time I went back to work at the high school, the situation had changed, but the war was not over. At school, the mood was sombre. The Grade 12 students, who were seventeen years old, were not in school. They had been sent to work in agriculture and other vital industries to replace the men who had gone to war. The Grade 11 students were in revolt because they had not been sent to help in the national effort, and they refused to study.

"We're not old enough to help in this emergency," one of my students said sarcastically. "We have to stay in school and study with all the little boys and girls."

"How can we concentrate on English verbs when there is a national emergency?" another boy said. "The very existence of Israel is in danger and you want us to study English grammar?" I did not know what to answer him.

So they didn't study English grammar; they each told stories about family members who had gone to fight and about their own experiences in the past two weeks.

Word was received that the boys' physical-education teacher had fallen in battle. Since I had been teaching at the school for only a month when the war broke out, I did not have a strong memory of him, just a vague recollection of a slim young man who had spoken out against excessive punishment at our first staff meeting. I learned that he had a wife and a small son. My heart ached for them all.

There was a feeling of solidarity and brotherly love among the population such as I had never witnessed before. Every evening on the television news, the names of the fallen were announced and the whole nation mourned them. Children sent parcels to soldiers at the front to boost their morale and show them that the entire nation was thinking of them. These parcels contained home-baked cookies, chocolate bars, nuts, magazines, cigarettes, playing cards, shaving cream and even socks and underwear. With each parcel, the sender included a letter wishing the recipient soldier good luck and a safe return home. Weeks later, Pnina and Shelly were very excited when they each received a letter from a soldier, thanking them for their parcels.

Mothers who had sons at the front sent them personal packages. One day, I heard instructions on the radio about what to send and especially what *not* to send in these parcels. It was a bit of comic relief to hear the announcer explain that chopped liver and gefilte fish could not be sent in the mail because they would spoil. When I related this to Tashie in the evening, he laughed. "What do you expect? It's a country of Jewish mothers."

People were nicer to each other on the street, on the bus, in stores. There was none of the pushing and the brashness that I had learned to live with (but not to accept) in my new home country. One morning when I was driving to work, I stopped at a red light. The driver behind me got out of his car with a rag in his hand and cleaned my back windshield. I was flabbergasted. Such a thing had never happened before, and I was quite sure it would never happen again.

In November, Israel and Egypt signed a ceasefire agreement. It took another two months to reach an agreement on the disengagement and separation of their respective forces at the Suez Canal front. A ceasefire between Israel and Syria was attained only at the end of May 1974.

The war that had begun in October was finally over, but it left cruel scars, some of them permanent, not only on the families of the numerous fallen and on the wounded, but also on the nation as a whole.

A Time of Sorrow

Our third child, Shlomit, was born in May of 1975. She brought a ray of sunshine into our family after the tensions of the Yom Kippur War. I spoke only English to her, so the older children were forced to speak to her in English as well. She did not know any Hebrew until she went to preschool at three and a half.

Then I began to teach English part-time at Seminar Hakibbutzim Teachers' College and two years later at Tel Aviv University in the preparatory year. I found teaching adults who were motivated to learn very satisfying.

So the years went. The children grew, I taught and Tashie worked for Israel Aircraft Industries. His work entailed a lot of travelling, so he was away from home for two or three weeks at a time. I was lonely at those times and the children protested his frequent absences, but they loved the presents that he always brought home from his trips.

On July 25, 1982, I received a phone call from Montreal. It was my cousin Sidney. "I… I'm so sorry to have to tell you this," he said. "Your father has died."

I was devastated. My father had had a heart attack before, but only a very mild one. My mother and I had both been more concerned with controlling his diabetes. Neither one of us thought that he might die so suddenly. My parents had finally bought a condominium not far from ours, planning to move to Israel eventually, and had stayed there with my aunt and uncle on one of their visits. And now this terrible blow, and the guilt of not being there to console my mother!

Tashie made all the arrangements for our flight. That same night our whole family but Pnina, who was in the army and only got permission to come several days later, flew to New York and from there to Montreal. I could not stop crying the whole way.

When we arrived in Montreal, we heard all the details of what had happened. On that Sunday morning, my mother had slept a little later than usual. When she awoke, she saw that my father was not in bed. This did not surprise her because he usually got up before her. She washed and dressed and then she called to my father. When he did not answer her, my mother thought that perhaps the TV in the den was on and he couldn't hear her. She called louder, but still there was no answer.

She went into the den and there sat Avrumeh, with his eyes closed and a peaceful expression on his face. She was surprised to see him dozing so early in the morning. "Avrumeh, Avrumeh, wake up," she said. But Avrumeh would wake no more. She shook him and screamed his name, but he was gone. She called a neighbour who called the emergency medical service, but all that the young doctor who arrived could do was to sign the death certificate.

The funeral was the next day, on Monday. When we were all ready to leave the house, my mother said, "Where is Avrumeh?" before she realized what she was saying. For forty-four years they had gone everywhere together, through terrible times and good times. It was hard for her to grasp that from now on, she would have to go on without him.

I held my mother's arm at the cemetery. I could feel her shudder when they lowered the coffin into the ground. I myself was numb. That was not my father any longer. My father was somewhere else, not there. My father was a memory in my head, a feeling in my heart.

For the seven days of shiva, family and friends visited to pay their respects and to comfort our family. It was a time of grief, but it was also a time of family solidarity and reunion with old friends and acquaintances, some of whom I, and even my mother, had not seen for a very long time. Many people told my mother to find consolation in the fact that Avrumeh had died so peacefully and did not suffer at all. "It was better this way," some said. But my mother insisted that it would have been better if he were still alive: "There is no 'better' when you're talking about death." Visitors streamed through the house every afternoon and evening. It was very tiring but also a great source of solace.

I remained in Montreal for a month. I helped my mother fold up all my father's clothes to give to charity, but I took a few things I wanted to keep for myself as mementos: a silk scarf, a mohair vest. I thought that I would wear these items myself and feel close to my father. My aunts and uncles stopped in every evening to be with my mother and they promised me that they would continue to come after I went home. After thirty days, there was a memorial service.

During the mourning period, more than one person asked my mother whether she would now move to Israel to be near her only daughter and her grandchildren. She always answered that it was too soon to make any decisions. I thought that my mother was very wise. A time of sorrow is not the time to make hasty plans that might be regretted later on.

Then the summer was over. The children had to go back to school and I had to go teach. With a heavy heart, I said goodbye to my mother and flew back to Israel.

During the next few days, I was very busy shopping for schoolbooks, notebooks and all the other paraphernalia that the children needed for school. I also had to get the house back in order after our sudden departure, to shop for food and to pay overdue bills. I spent a great deal of time on the telephone, as the Israeli relatives and friends called to express their condolences and to ask the details of my father's death and of my mother's coping with the new situation. As busy as I was, whenever it was quiet, I could hear the voice of a child crying. It took me days to realize that the voice I was hearing was my own. For me, the summer of 1982 was a cursed season.

I worried constantly about my mother. How was she managing on her own? How was she dealing with her loneliness? I knew that my mother's two sisters, her brother and their spouses provided a strong support system for her, but still, they all went home each evening while my mother remained alone. I felt helpless and guilty for being so far away. But I also knew that my mother was a very strong woman who would brave whatever circumstances fate had sent her way, as she always had in the past.

I pleaded with my mother to come to Israel, at least for a visit, but my mother would not hear of it. She would not go anywhere during the year of mourning. So, during the fall semester break at the university, I went with Shlomit, who was then seven and a half years old, to spend two weeks with my mother.

My mother was very glad to have us there and she invited all the aunts and uncles the very first evening. Sidney and his wife, Annie, were there too. It was good to see all the relatives again.

When everyone had left and we had cleaned up the dishes, my mother told me that she had a doctor's appointment in two days and that she would really like me to come with her. She told me it was just a routine check-up.

On the day of the medical appointment, after we had eaten an early lunch, my mother said, "It's not my family doctor I'm going to see. It's a specialist."

"What kind of specialist?" I asked.

"I found a tiny lump in my breast," my mother answered, "and I'm going to this specialist to find out what it is." She hadn't told me earlier, she said, because she didn't want me to worry.

The doctor's office was in the Jewish General Hospital. When I exited the elevator and saw the Oncology Department sign, I shuddered.

After examining my mother, the doctor performed a needle biopsy to determine whether or not the lump was malignant, and she and I waited in the examining room for the results. At last he came back into the room. He told us that the lump was malignant and would have to be removed along with some of the lymph tissue in the armpit.

I burst into tears, but my mother was in perfect control of her emotions. I thought that perhaps my mother, because of her imperfect English, had not understood what "malignant" meant. But my mother immediately disproved that assumption. "It's cancer, doctor, yes?" she asked. Her mind was, as always, five steps ahead of everyone else's. "Please make the operation as soon as possible. My daughter lives in Israel and she is here only for two weeks. I want very much to have the operation while she is here."

The surgery took place five days later. Before they took my mother into the operating room, she said to me, "I want you to know, Chanale, that if I don't wake up, it's all right. I lived a long life, I survived Hitler, I saw you grow up and marry a nice man and have nice children. And now Papa is gone. If my time is up, I'm ready."

"Mama," I said, "stop talking nonsense! You're going to be all right. It's not a very serious operation and you have a very good chance of recovery. I'll be right here waiting for you." I kissed my mother and said, "Good luck! I'll see you in a few hours."

As I sat in the waiting room outside the operating rooms, I tried not to think of what was being done to my mother or of what lay ahead for both of us. But my thoughts seemed to have a will of their own and came unbidden into my mind. I found only a bit of distraction in some coffee and cookies, in a magazine; it was difficult to concentrate.

Finally, the doctor came out of the operating room. He told me that everything had gone well; he was sure they got all of it. When I first saw my mother, she was still asleep, and when she started to come out of the anesthetic, she said a lot of things that made no sense to me. And then she slept some more. The first thing she said on waking was, "I guess I woke up after all. What a surprise!"

"Oh, Mama," I said. I never knew how to react when my mother spoke about her own death.

She recovered according to schedule and after a week, she was sent home. I phoned my family in Israel and made arrangements to stay an extra week because I could not leave my mother immediately after the surgery. Tashie, who had been in South America for his work, flew through Montreal and took Shlomit home with him.

My mother would still need some radiation treatments, and though it bothered me terribly that I would not be there to accompany her to her treatments, my aunts and uncle promised to take good care of her. I knew that they would. They were all very devoted to each other and I certainly appreciated that, but I was going back to Israel with an uneasy heart. When I was in Canada, I worried about my children in Israel; when I was in Israel, I worried about my mother in Canada.

In the summer of 1983, our whole family went to Montreal for the unveiling of my father's tombstone. The following summer, my mother came to Israel and stayed with us for six weeks. A little while later, a letter arrived. Apparently after she had gotten back to Montreal my mother had done some serious thinking. "I have decided to move to Israel," she wrote. "When I was visiting you, I was also trying out life in Israel, imagining if I could live there. Yes, I think I could adjust to life in Israel; I have adjusted to much worse in my lifetime. But the last thing I would want is to be a burden to you and Tashie, so I will not accept Tashie's kind invitation to come live with you. I would like to live in my apartment, the one Papa and I bought."

So in the summer of 1985, three years after my father's death, I went to Montreal to help my mother pack up her possessions, move out of her house, then bring her to Israel with me. It was not the way I would have written the script. I had wanted both my parents to come live in Israel, but at least my mother had come, and of her own free will.

The Gulf War

Between 1990 and 1991, yet another war affected us — the infamous Gulf War, which began in the late summer of 1990. Iraq invaded Kuwait and threatened to attack Israel as well, so all of a sudden we had to prepare for the possibility of a chemical attack, which meant we had to know how to seal one room in our houses, to make the room airtight. My son, David, who had been out of the army for over two years, was now working as a firefighter for the city of Tel Aviv; he was the one who, in August, had told us what we should prepare in order to be ready, to the extent that one could ever be ready. We needed masking tape to seal the windows; sheets of plastic to tape over the windows, the air conditioner and any other openings; a pair of scissors; baking soda to dissolve in water and use for soaking towels to stuff under the door; bottled water to last for several days, if necessary; canned food, a can opener and cutlery in a closed glass jar; a flashlight and batteries, in case the electricity went out; a portable radio in order to listen to instructions, and extra batteries; books, playing cards and games, in case we had to spend a long time in the room. If the government thought that the situation warranted it, the whole population would be supplied with gas masks. I had turned pale at the thought of this frightening prospect.

Then, in October 1990, Israelis were issued protective kits, each containing a gas mask with an attachable filter, a small container of medicated powder to apply to the skin in case of burns caused by contact with gas, gauze pads to remove the powder and a syringe containing atropine, only to be injected if there were symptoms of exposure to nerve gas. At the centres where the kits were distributed, explanations were given as to when and how to use these various items, a film was shown illustrating their use and there was an opportunity to try on a gas mask. Everyone was told again and again not to open the kits unless instructed to do so. It was a frightening experience but everyone accepted it stoically. People had been fairly confident that the time to use the kits would never come.

And then, three months later, in January 1991, we were instructed to seal a room. I phoned my mother. She had been extremely anxious about the possibility of war breaking out ever since the crisis began in August. Her experiences in Poland during the Holocaust had left their indelible marks on all her thoughts and actions. In view of the deteriorating situation, I asked her to come move in with Tashie and me. At first she refused, but after some negotiating she agreed to come on Tuesday, January 15. That was the deadline that the United Nations had set, after which a coalition of armies led by the United States could use force against Iraq if its leader, Saddam Hussein, did not pull his armies out of Kuwait.

The day came and went and the whole world waited to see what would happen next. On the Israeli television channels, public service announcements were broadcast from time to time, explaining what people should do in case an alarm was sounded. Unlike in other wars, the population was instructed to go not into their bomb shelters but into their sealed rooms, where they were to tape the doors shut and put on their gas masks. Gas masks for children came in various sizes and designs, right down to the *mamat*, which was like a plastic crib in which a baby could be totally enclosed, with an air filter and a mechanism for giving the baby a bottle. I was glad I had no small children or grandchildren to worry about at this stressful time. My youngest daughter, Shlomit, spoke with a calm authority that belied her fifteen and a half years, and several times had demonstrated how to put on a gas mask and had helped her grandmother get into hers. I was so proud of her.

The war began that night — well, early the next morning, really. I didn't know whether I wanted the war to start or not. I only knew that I didn't want to sit and wait day after day, with the tension growing continuously.

We turned on the radio and lay awake for hours, listening. American, British and Saudi Arabian airplanes were bombing various strategic locations in Iraq, including Baghdad, its capital. Apparently, there was no resistance from Iraq except for the firing of anti-aircraft guns. Nonetheless, everyone was instructed to stay home in case of an attack on Israel. We spent the day watching television and from then on we lived from newscast to newscast.

On January 18, Israel was attacked by missiles. We heard the wail of the sirens, which meant we had to go into our sealed rooms and put on our gas masks. Once in the room, I looked at my mother. She was sitting absolutely still, not moving at all. I grew frightened. "Are you all right, Mama?" I asked. "Can you breathe?" My mother's voice sounded muffled and strange through the mask, but then she nodded her head and I was reassured. At that moment, I was very glad that we had practised putting on the gas masks.

Forty minutes later, which seemed like many hours, the radio announcer told us to remove the gas masks but to remain in the sealed rooms. Eventually, we were allowed to emerge.

Essential work would continue as usual, according to the announcements, but everyone else was to stay home. All supermarkets and food stores were open. I went out to buy a few things. Everyone was carrying his or her kit, as per instructions. People were discussing their experiences of the night before.

There was that feeling of closeness that enveloped all the inhabitants of Israel whenever there was a major crisis. Suddenly, each person was his brother's keeper. I had felt it in the Yom Kippur War and now I felt it again. I was hoping that Israel would stay out of the war.

And so the days went: attacks, sirens, sealed doors, gas masks. Tashie and I were beginning to feel claustrophobic from being in the house so much. Once, we walked down to the beach, which took about twenty minutes. It was a beautiful day but the beach was totally deserted. I had walked here on cold, cloudy winter days, but never had I seen it so empty.

After six days, everyone went back to work, but the schools were still closed, and most of the universities declared their first semester over one week earlier than scheduled. I was therefore on my semester break, which was just as well since I could not imagine leaving my terrified mother alone in the house under the circumstances. I would go out to the store to buy some food while Shlomit stayed with her grandmother. We all stayed home all the time, and for lack of any other activity, we kept cooking and eating.

So we continued living in this surrealistic manner. Except for the first Saturday, all the attacks occurred during the evening or at night. As a result, nobody went out in the evenings unless it was absolutely necessary. People finished work around four o'clock so that they could get home before dark. There were big traffic jams leaving Tel Aviv between 4:00 p.m. and 6:00 p.m. because many people who worked in Tel Aviv were now sleeping elsewhere. All entertainment events were cancelled. A few restaurants and pubs were open in the evening, but most were closed. Some people were going out to cafés and restaurants during the day; we did not go anywhere. We were waiting for this strange war to be over.

Shlomit finally went back to school. She was delighted to see all her classmates, but they did not learn very much the first day. Teachers were busy preparing their classrooms for a possible gas attack and comparing stories of their adventures so far.

Sometimes two whole days would pass without an attack, sometimes as many as five days. Then, just as people would begin to think that perhaps the war was over for Israel, Saddam Hussein would send us a reminder that we were still in the war. Sometimes there were even two attacks in one night. The country sustained a lot of damage; many people were injured and some were killed.

I went back to teach, and it was wonderful to see my students again. Nothing serious had happened to any of them — they told me that one of the girls had some damage to her house, but no one had been hurt. That student was not living in her house now and she did not come to class. In my second class, all the students were there. It also felt wonderful to teach again, to do what I loved to do, and to feel some degree of normalcy returning to my life.

It was now a month since the war had begun, and the number of missiles that had fallen on Israel was approximately thirty-five, quite a few more than the one or two that had been predicted by the experts before the war began. I was getting tired of it all.

One night, after two missile attacks, it was just too much for me, and I cracked. At 3:30 in the morning, I was in my mother's room, trying to wake her, and it suddenly occurred to me what a bizarre situation this was. Why should I have to wake my poor, elderly mother in the middle of the night to put on a gas mask? Didn't my mother suffer enough during World War II? I felt like crying, but I didn't because there was too much to do. When we went out to the stairway, our neighbours were already there. Their youngest son, who was three and a half years old, was crying. The other two children were grumpy. I thought it was cruel to disturb the sleep of innocent children. Later, when I was back in my bed, I broke down and wept for a very long time. Tashie did not know how to comfort me. At 5:30 a.m., during the second alarm, I was back to my usual controlled and efficient self.

And then suddenly, at the end of February, it was over! When Iraq agreed to accept all the United Nations resolutions, the United States declared a ceasefire. Israelis were instructed to remove the plastic sheets and tape from their sealed rooms and to carefully pack away their gas masks in case they were needed again sometime in the future. We could now go back to living a normal life.

Because it had happened so fast, it was hard to believe that the nightmare had ended. After six weeks of extreme tension and thirty-nine Scud missiles, it was finally over.

It was Purim at the time, the joyous holiday of masks and costumes. In Israel, Purim that year was a double holiday. Many people were out in the streets, without their gas masks. Children in costumes were everywhere. There was a feeling of jubilation in the air, and I knew that I would never forget that Purim.

An Emotional Journey

My mother used to correspond with Panie Krynska, the woman in whose farm we had hidden during the war. When our family got settled in Montreal, my mother would send her parcels of clothing, and Panie Krynska would write to my mother to thank her and to tell her what was happening on the farm. Eventually her son, Heniek, took over the correspondence with my mother. Heniek did not remain on the farm; he moved several times, from one large city to another, before moving back to the village of Morze. One day, he wrote to my mother, asking her to please stop writing to him because her letters were getting him into trouble. He also asked my mother to destroy his letter. It was not clear to us whether receiving letters from Canada was getting him into trouble with the Communist authorities or whether he did not want his neighbours to know about their correspondence. In any case, my mother stopped writing to him and we lost contact. Even if Heniek had wanted to contact us after Poland was freed from Communist rule in 1989, he would not have known where to find us, since from 1985 my mother had lived in Israel.

My dear auntie Henia, the mother of my cousin Sidney, had corresponded continually with the family that had sheltered them. When she became very ill, Sidney took over the correspondence. By then, the parents of the Polish family had passed away, and the one who continued to write was Zigmund, the young shepherd boy they had met in the woods on that fateful day in 1943. Sidney had fond memories of him; they had threshed wheat together, done various chores together and even played cards together. His renewed connection with Zigmund Krynski (unrelated to the Krynskis who saved us) caused him to think about visiting Poland. In 1996, my aunt died, and Sidney began to talk to me about visiting Poland. He somehow felt that it was his duty to do so.

I had always vowed that I would never go back to Poland. I had no good memories of Poland and did not feel any nostalgia for the place where I was born. Although Sidney and I had been close throughout our lives, visiting each other in Montreal and Israel, when Sidney told me that he and Annie were definitely going to Poland my first reaction was, "Have a safe trip. I'm not interested."

But then I began to rethink the matter. Sidney is seven years older than I am. He remembers many things that I don't. I thought to myself that if I ever changed my mind and went to Poland without him, I would not know what to look for. The truth is that I was afraid of what my emotional reaction would be if I went back to the place where I had spent my early years.

When I decided to go, I insisted that my husband, Tashie, come with me, even though he had a very negative attitude to this project. I explained to him that I needed him there to pick up the pieces in case I fell apart. When our son, David, heard about the trip, he said, "I'm coming, too."

I tried to tell my mother about the trip, but as soon as I started saying that Sidney was going to Poland, she immediately cut me off, exclaiming, "Tell him not to go!" My mother was not in the best of health by then, and she was perhaps confusing the past with the present, but she was still very afraid of antisemitism in Poland. She kept saying, "Remember what happened to us there? Tell him not to go!" I didn't have the heart to be honest with her, so I told her I was going to Copenhagen, which was partly true, since it would be part of my itinerary.

In 1997, Sidney's son Larry, who would be coming with us, spent a few months planning our trip. My second cousin Shoshana Licht

Bentman, who was born in Israel but whose parents came from Semiatych and were also Holocaust survivors, announced that she and her husband, Igal, wanted to join us. Another couple that would take part in this journey was Sidney's stepbrother Simon Braitman, a survivor of Auschwitz, and his wife, Josephine.

With great trepidation, I set out on this trip back to the place of my birth.

On Thursday, September 11, 1997, we all arrived in Warsaw from different places: Sidney, Annie and Larry from Montreal; Simon and Josephine from Rochester, New York; Shoshana and Igal on one flight from Israel; and Tashie, David and I on another.

The next day, all ten of us set out bright and early in a van with a driver and our Polish guide, Chris, on our way to Siemiatycze, known to us as Semiatych. The first thing that Chris said was that he knew, from previous meetings with survivors, that we had a very negative view of Poland, that we thought all Poles collaborated with the Germans during the war and that he wanted to prove to us that there were good Poles as well.

Our first stop was at the home of Stanislaw, the son of Zigmund Krynski, whose parents had hidden Sidney and his parents during the war. Stanislaw (called Staszek) lived with his wife and little girl in a new housing project for young families on the edge of the town. Actually, it was the site of the former ghetto, of which nothing now remained.

After that, we went to the Jewish cemetery of Siemiatycze, which was nearby. A large stone plaque had been placed over the mass grave of seventy Jews who had been shot while running away from the ghetto on the last night before the liquidation began, the night of November 1–2, 1942. After the war, my uncle Shieh (Joshua) Kejles had reburied them according to Jewish tradition. One of the people buried there is his father and my grandfather, Ephraim (Froikeh) Kejles. The plaque, all in Polish, shows my grandfather's and uncle's names very prominently written, as well as those of a few others. We lit candles and placed Israeli flags on the mass grave.

Broken tombstones, their shards plastered together in a long strip in an attempt at preservation, were all that remained otherwise. Almost all the other tombstones had been removed for building material or paving stones during the war or after. As we walked through the rest of the cemetery, we found small remnants of tombstones, too small to be useful for even those purposes. The fence around the cemetery still stood, as well as the arches at the entrance, but the wrought-iron gates were missing. (A few years later I learned that through the efforts and funding of former Semiatych Jews these had been replaced.)

We then went to explore Siemiatycze. Parts of it looked like they did before the war — small, weather-beaten wooden or brick houses with small yards. Other sections were prettier, newer, renovated or rebuilt. Staszek showed us a house that, he'd been told, had belonged to my grandfather Lisogurski. But was this really the house where Sidney and I and our parents had lived for a few months after we'd been liberated, before we had left Poland? I thought it was too small and too modern, and I had always imagined it as a much larger house. I couldn't really say that I remembered it, and I was surprised that Sidney did not, either. We tried to find elderly people to confirm that this was the house, but we weren't able to.

After that we went to the "Broom," the large square in the centre of town. It was a park surrounded by quite decent attached two-storey buildings, the ground floors containing stores and the upper floors consisting of living quarters with wrought-iron balconies. Before the war, the area had also contained buildings that had been built hundreds of years earlier, but these had all been destroyed during the German occupation.

Before we had been forced into the ghetto, my family, as well as Sidney's family, had lived in the houses facing the Broom, and with the help of a photograph, Sidney succeeded in identifying his house, and he told me that my parents and I lived three or four houses down. I looked at those houses, and I realized that I had been born in one of them, and I felt...nothing. Sidney took us into the lane behind those houses and told us that he had played there with his friends, and that they had sometimes climbed over the fence to pick apples from the trees belonging to the church. That was very moving.

We also visited the synagogue, which is now a cultural centre. The main hall is used as a theatre. I thought about how my maternal and paternal grandparents, uncles, aunts and cousins must have prayed in that building. Upstairs, the separate women's section, now an art gallery, was exhibiting paintings by a Polish artist of Jews being persecuted by the Germans, drawn from his memories as an eyewitness. But I felt that there were problems with two of these paintings — in one, all the Jews were dressed in Hasidic clothing and the men had sidelocks, which was not true of the Jewish majority in Semiatych in the late 1930s. Another painting portrayed Jews being forced by Germans to bury a statue of Lenin in the Jewish cemetery, but we had heard from our parents that this had been perpetrated by the local Poles and not by the Germans.

The Talmud Torah religious school used to be next to the synagogue; it now housed a kindergarten and a library.

Our next stop was in the village of Krynki-Sobole at Zigmund Krynski's house. His parents had hidden Sidney and his parents. Zigmund and his wife were expecting us and received us warmly. When Zigmund and Sidney embraced, my tears began to flow. They had been young boys who had worked and played together. He and his wife were now living in the same house where his parents had lived, and they showed us the places where the Zoltaks had hidden and the barn where the wheat had been threshed and the well from which they still drew water. It was very emotional and we all cried, including our Polish guide and the driver. Zigmund's wife had prepared a big lunch for all of us on her wood-fired stove. We really enjoyed the food and meeting these people.

We asked Zigmund if he knew where Heniek Krynski was. He told us that Heniek had moved back to Morze. Zigmund wanted to take us there, but his son, Staszek, advised him against it. Having hidden Jews during the war was not considered a badge of honour among these people and they still kept it a secret. Even after fifty-three years, it still created bad feelings and jealousy among neighbours who thought, erroneously, that rescuers were better off than they were because the Jews they had saved had left them many things.

Staszek took us there but never left the van.

As we drove up to the house, we saw an elderly man working in the yard and an ancient-looking woman came out.

Sidney said to the man in Polish, "Are you Heniek Krynski?"

"Yes," he said.

Sidney asked, "Do you remember a family named Lisogurski?"

"Yes," he answered.

Sidney asked, "How do you know them?"

"They were here. Rachela Lisogurski."

Sidney pointed at me and said, "This is Rachela's daughter."

The old woman cried out, "Chania!"

She was Heniek's older sister, Gienia, the one who had been married at the time we were there and who hadn't known about us because the Krynskis didn't trust her husband. She had never laid eyes on me, so I was astonished that she knew my name. She later explained that after the war, her mother had talked a lot about us.

Heniek and I hugged and kissed each other, and then I introduced him to Tashie and David as our family's cameras and video cameras were rolling and the tears were flowing. Heniek told us that his parents' house and the barn under which we had been hidden, about a kilometre away, no longer existed. He had moved in with his widowed sister, Gienia, when his house fell apart. The house they lived in now was very small and extremely bare. I don't think they had electricity. I asked about his younger sister Krysia, who'd been a few years older than me; he said she was dead but didn't provide any more particulars. I also asked him about Vera, my mother's "friend" who had refused to return my mother's goods to her during the war, and he told me that she was also dead. I must admit that I had a feeling of satisfaction because at that point my mother was still alive.

I had not thought that I would have much chance of meeting Heniek, so this whole experience was very surprising, gratifying and emotional.

After this, we drove through Grodzisk and were shown a house that had belonged to our grandfather Ephraim and grandmother Rivka. During the rest of our stay in Poland, we visited Białystok, Auschwitz and Treblinka, the camp where the Jews from our town were murdered.

Nothing at Auschwitz shocked us. We had all read books and seen photographs and movies. Being there gave me a feeling of the enormity of the place and of how helpless an individual would have felt there. I cried, but I wasn't hysterical. I didn't fall apart.

At Treblinka, there is no trace of the camp left; the Germans destroyed everything before the end of the war. The memorial there is abstract and symbolic, a massive structure created from huge slabs of stone. Beyond the large abstract monument are thousands of upright stones of varying sizes (*matzevot* in Hebrew, tombstones or monuments), which have names of communities engraved on them and to me seemed arranged in rows like the crossties in a railroad track. We could not find the name Siemiatycze, neither on the indexed map at the entrance nor among the stones themselves. The whole place evoked in me a feeling of sadness rather than horror, except that I frequently found myself wondering what the earth beneath my feet was hiding. As I walked there, I felt as though the earth on which I was treading contained the blood and the bones of my family.

I wasn't disappointed by the lack of anything there because I had been told what to expect. At the very least, I knew that this was the place where my father's parents, sister and brothers and their families were taken to, as well as my uncle Shieh's wife, Chana, and their two daughters, Chayale and Yentale, and other cousins and relatives whose names I don't even know. Whether they perished there or were transferred elsewhere I have no way of knowing, because none of them came back. But in that place, even with no visible remnant of the evil that had been perpetrated there, I thought of them all.

Of our group only Tashie, David and I went to Białystok, to look for my grandmother Rivka's grave in the Jewish cemetery. After we had left Poland in 1945, my uncle Shieh had put a stone on her grave and sent us photos of it. Before our trip, I had contacted Shimon Bartnowski, "the last Jew in Białystok," as he called himself, and asked him to find my grandmother's grave. I'd sent him copies of the pictures of the grave and money to hire people who could read Hebrew letters. He had told me on the phone that this particular cemetery had been totally vandalized and that there wouldn't be much hope of finding any marked grave, but I insisted on looking for myself.

We arrived at Mr. Bartnowski's small apartment and he took us to the cemetery. It was just as he had described it: two or three ancient tombs of famous rabbis, a large monument to many people who had died in an epidemic, but the rest was devastation — small pieces of broken gravestones and wild vegetation. It was very sad to see, but there are many cemeteries like that in Poland, and indeed in other Eastern European countries. To me, all of Poland is one big Jewish cemetery. Nevertheless, I was glad that I had come. Somewhere there my grandmother lies buried, and I came to honour her memory.

As we'd been driving back from Auschwitz on our last day with Chris, our guide, I had felt it important to conclude the discussion he had started on the very first day, when he'd expressed his concern that we Jews tended to accuse all Poles of having collaborated with the Nazis in killing Jews. He had told us that we must not forget that there had been good Poles even then. I'd answered him that of course, this group was very well aware of the good Poles because without them, some of us in this van would not have survived, but the fact remained that many Poles helped the Nazis. Now, on that last day, I went up to the front of the van and asked him what young Polish people were taught about this period in their history. He admitted that they were not taught about Polish antisemitism or of any overt acts during and after the war. I told him that I could not blame anyone for not wanting to risk their life and the life of their family in order to save mine, but that I did blame all those who had reported Jews to the Germans or had killed Jews themselves during and even after the war. I told him that such acts were well-documented and could not be denied. I then gave him a copy of *Out of the Depths*, my mother's book, which we had used as our reference book during the trip. He thanked me and asked me whether he could quote from it to other visitors. I told him that he was free to use it.

During my emotional meeting with Heniek Krynski, my husband, Tashie, had said that we should give him some money. So at that time our son, David, went into his house, with our guide as interpreter, and told Heniek that he wanted to thank him for saving his mother, noting that, otherwise, he would not have come into the world, and giving him a few hundred dollars.

After that, I would send Heniek money every Christmas, and he would write me beautiful letters, thanking me profusely and explaining that his only other income was a meagre government pension, so the money I sent him, which came to a huge sum in Polish zloty, made his life easier. The woman who translated the letters for me told me that for a man who had grown up on a farm and presumably had no higher education, Heniek's written Polish was very elegant, and I could see for myself that his handwriting was very delicate.

When I returned from Poland, I told my mother about my trip. It had been intense, meaningful and just good for our family members to be together, to laugh and cry together, and to fill in bits of the story that is our family's heritage. I said to her that we should apply to Yad Vashem, Israel's museum and memorial to the victims of the Holocaust, to name Heniek and his parents as Righteous Among the Nations. Yad Vashem recognizes and honours gentiles who, at personal risk and without a financial or evangelistic motive, chose to save their Jewish neighbours from the ongoing genocide. My mother replied, "You do it after I am gone." I think that she did not want to be forced to delve into her memories of the war.

My mother died the following year, August 1998, at eighty-seven years old. Her health had declined over the previous seven years — she'd had to have one hip replaced and then the other, and surgery to remove a growth in her colon; she had recovered from each of these operations gradually, and each time, more slowly. It was difficult for her to walk and then her memory began to fail.

I didn't want my mother to sleep alone in her apartment and she didn't want to stay in my house. She said that as long as she lived in her own house she felt independent, so we brought in a series of students who slept in her apartment rent-free, just so there would be someone in the house with her.

Then my mother began to suffer from terrible pains in her legs. The doctor said that it was from osteoporosis. The pills he prescribed reduced the pain but increased her dementia. She screamed during the night and the student-caregiver could not sleep. We hired another caregiver because one could not manage. My mother took morphine in liquid form, which she called "vodka." And then one day she died.

It was not an elegant end to a very eventful life. I consoled myself with the thought that she had survived the Holocaust, had found joy in her daughter and son-in-law, in her three grandchildren and three great-grandchildren.

⌒

Why didn't I apply to Yad Vashem after my mother's death? Who knows? I was busy with life.

Heniek Krynski died in 2005. Sidney sent me an email that he had been informed by Zigmund, through his son. I was now the only one left of that circle, and I found myself crying. For whom? For Heniek? For all of us who had lived through that nightmare? Heniek had never married and had no children, at least none that I knew about; Krysia, his younger sister, had died long before. That was the end of that chapter — or so I thought.

Honouring Courage
and Compassion

In May 2013, I had a big surprise. My cousin Sidney Zoltak received an email that said, "I am looking for Mrs. Chana Broder," which he of course forwarded to me. The sender was a young woman named Izabella Wierzbicka, who explained that she was the granddaughter of Krystina (Krysia) Krynska. She had recently heard that her grandmother and her great-grandparents had saved Jews during World War II and she wanted to know more. It seems that, in Poland, it was now not only legitimate to have saved Jews, but it was actually a source of pride.

Izabella had heard from her aunt that her great-grandparents had sheltered Jews during the war. When she asked her mother about it, her mother said that she did not know, but one of her uncles affirmed that it was true. She then set out on a search to find the Jews who had been saved by her family. This could not have been an easy task. I know that she used the internet — she told me that she had read an article online that I had written for the Canadian Museum of Immigration at Pier 21, in Halifax. Also, my cousin Sidney had been in Siemiatycze several times since I had been there with him, and he had probably left his email address with the local historian, who publishes a weekly paper. The Reverend Paweł Rytel-Andrianik, who comes from our area in Poland and whom I had met in Israel, also had a part in the process. This reverend had known the wartime priest of Siemiatycze, and when the reverend was in Israel to work on his doctorate, he came to the meetings I went to of former Semiatych Jews. When I told him my story, he helped to find the family's descendants when he was back in Siemiatycze. So, eventually, Izabella found me.

Since then we have exchanged many emails. She told me that her grandmother Krysia had given birth to eight children and had died of cancer at the early age of forty-eight. Izabella was born after her grandmother's death. She was born in Brussels, where both her parents worked at the time, but now she was living in Poland, in Białystok. I told Izabella our story and the part that her great-grand-parents played in it, and I sent her a copy of my mother's book.

Izabella had a limited knowledge of English and she used Google Translate to write to me. Although I had spoken Polish as a child, I have forgotten my Polish and only recall certain words. I cannot follow a conversation in Polish and certainly cannot speak it. But Izabella and I managed to understand each other.

In 2014, I applied to Yad Vashem to award the title of Righteous Among the Nations to the Krynski family, and my application was approved about a year later. After this process, Yad Vashem contacted Izabella's aunt Zdzislawa Chlebowska, who worked in Brussels, and she agreed to receive the honour. I called Zdzislawa and we spoke in French. Mine was very rusty, but I managed to understand that the whole family was proud of what her grandparents had done during the war, and that they would be happy to receive the award. She also said that she was anxious to meet me and that my whole family and I would be welcome in her house in Siemiatycze. I also spoke to Izabella on the phone with the help of a friend who speaks Polish.

I was then in touch with the Israeli embassy in Warsaw in order to designate a time and a place for the ceremony. Because my three children and their spouses wanted to come to this ceremony and so did the older grandchildren, we had to consider everyone's schedules — school, army, vacations — and we finally settled on May 2016. Formerly, these ceremonies took place either at Yad Vashem in Jerusalem or at the Israeli embassy in Warsaw. Now, if the ceremony is to take place in Poland, it is performed in the vicinity of where the people were hidden or saved. I think this gives the local towns publicity and the pride that now comes from proving that they were helpers. I stress the word "now" because not too long ago, as I mentioned, it was not considered a point of pride to have helped Jews, and those who had done so kept silent about their actions.

The ceremony was set for May 24, 2016, in Siemiatycze. The title of Righteous Among the Nations would be granted by Yad Vashem to Konstanty and Bronislawa Krynski and their children, Henryk (Heniek) and Krystina (Krysia) and awarded by the Ambassador of Israel to Poland. Since the Krynskis had passed away, the award would be accepted on their behalf by their eldest granddaughter, Zdzislawa Chlebowska, who came home from Brussels especially for the ceremony.

I went to Siemiatycze with my daughter Pnina, her husband, Navot, and their son Ohad, my son David, his wife, Carmel, and their daughter Mika, and my younger daughter Shlomit, who lives in Toronto. Her partner, Michal, stayed home to care for their three young children, Amit, Alma and Noam. My husband, Tashie, who was not well, was not able to make the trip. My two other Israeli grandsons, Eitan and Yonatan, were also not able to come with us.

Late one morning, one day before the ceremony, we arrived in Siemiatycze. Because I had been there in 1997, I was able to show my family where I had lived with my parents before the war and the street where my father's family had lived.

We had arranged to meet at Zdzislawa's home. Although she and her family had agreed to receive the award, and I knew that fourteen of their family members would attend, we did not know how they would receive us. We were totally amazed when they greeted us outside with hugs and kisses (three kisses on the cheeks) and some of the men even kissed the ladies' hands, European style. Izabella's aunt Zdzislawa, a spunky woman, was very enthusiastic.

As we walked into the house, they lined up and sang *Sto Lat*, which is sung on festive occasions and means "A Hundred Years." We responded with the festive song *Hevenu Shalom Aleichem*, which means "We Brought Peace to You." The table was set and we partook of herring, devilled eggs, latkes and cakes. None of our party spoke Polish, so our driver was the interpreter and Izabella had also hired a translator from Siemiatycze. Izabella also understood English and spoke it haltingly, so we managed some kind of conversation.

From there, we went to the Jewish cemetery where my grandfather Ephraim Kejles is buried. From my visit in 1997, I knew that only a large, flat gravestone remained over the mass grave. I had originally thought that this would be a private visit, but before we left Israel, I received word that the Chief Rabbi of Poland, Michael Schudrich, and the Israeli Ambassador to Poland, Anna Azari, would be there. It turned out that representatives of both churches, Catholic and Eastern Orthodox, the mayor of the town and other officials were also there, and the descendants of the Krynski family also came along. We were surprised to see that a police car had closed off the street. There were lots of still and video cameras.

I explained briefly who was buried there, and we lit two memorial candles, one for my grandfather and one for all the others. Then the rabbi read *Tehillim* (Psalms) and sang *El Maleh Rachamim*, the memorial prayer for the souls of those who have passed. My three children and I said Kaddish. It was a very meaningful and emotional experience for me and the children.

Following this, we went to the cultural centre, formerly the synagogue, where the Righteous Among the Nations ceremony was to take place. How symbolic! In the building where my parents and grandparents had once prayed, those who had saved our lives during the Holocaust were going to be honoured.

After a few greetings, Emil, the young man who organized the ceremony for the embassy, explained why we were there and introduced me. I had prepared a speech at home and someone in my son's office had translated it into Polish. Now I read one paragraph in English, and Emil was able to read it immediately in Polish.

I told them that I was there to fulfill a long-overdue duty, to honour the saintly family that had saved my life, the lives of my parents,

Rachela and Abraham Lisogurski, and that of my grandmother Rivka Kejles. I briefly recounted how we had escaped from the ghetto on the night of November 2, 1942, and thus avoided being sent to the Treblinka death camp. I explained how we had come to the Krynskis in May of 1943. I told them that Pan Krynski had agreed to keep us on a trial basis for two weeks, but that when the two weeks were up, he did not have the heart to send us away.

I was very young at the time, I told them, but my parents had later told me that the Krynskis had helped many Jewish people before us. Nobody had lived there permanently, but Jews would stop in their house to rest, to get something to eat or perhaps to sleep over in the barn.

By sheltering us, I told the audience, the Krynskis had taken a terrible risk. If Polish people were caught helping Jews their whole family would be killed. It was an extremely courageous step to take, to put oneself and one's children in danger in order to help strangers. And yet, the Krynskis had taken this compassionate step.

I told them about our liberation, our move to Canada and then Israel, and how my mother had corresponded with both Panie Krynska and Heniek for a time. I also told them about our 1997 visit to Poland and my emotional reunion with Heniek, and our subsequent correspondence until his death in 2005. Because Heniek had not told me that Krysia had children, I hadn't known there were other family members I could have been in contact with.

I gave credit to Izabella Wierzbicka for doing the research and finding me on the internet, which was not easy. We have been corresponding by email since then and I feel that we are almost family. Thanks to her, we were able to grant the honour to the Krynski family, which they so richly deserve and which took so many years to come to fruition.

I introduced the members of my family who had come with me to this ceremony. I stressed the fact that if the Krynskis had not saved me, many of these people would not have been born.

Finally, I told them that when I wrote my story to Izabella, she responded that I had used very beautiful words to describe her great-grandparents. I responded that there were no words in any language beautiful enough to describe what her family had done for us. They risked their lives and the lives of their children to save us. What could be more beautiful than that? They were truly righteous people because they did what they believed to be right. I expressed the wish that their memory be blessed.

When I finished, I noticed that some members of the Krynski family were wiping tears from their eyes. Then both the ambassador and Zdzislawa were called to the stage and the medal and the certificate were given to her. She was very excited and spoke a few words of thanks. She and other family members repeatedly told us that they were thrilled that we had not forgotten what their forebears had done for us. We then hugged and kissed and posed for many pictures.

Next, we climbed into our van and they climbed into their cars, and they took us to the place in Morze where the Krynski house had stood and where the barn and the bunker in which we'd hidden had been. Nothing was left but an empty field. But this was still very exciting for me because I had not been there on my first trip back. We continued on to the Catholic cemetery, where their family is buried, side by side, and lit memorial candles for the people who had saved our lives. Finally, at my daughter Pnina's request, we drove through Grodzisk, the village where my mother was born and grew up, the place she used to tell Pnina about when she was little.

In the evening, we had a dinner for both families in Siemiatycze's main hotel. There was a lot of conversation with the help of the translators. Finally, we said goodbye in the parking lot amid a lot of hugs and kisses and promises to keep in touch and mutual invitations to visit.

It was a very emotional day, a magical day, above and beyond all our expectations. I feel a great sense of satisfaction that I accomplished this morally necessary deed.

Tashie

Tashie worked for Israel Aircraft Industries (IAI) for twenty-five years, the first twenty in the legal department. After a few years, he was put in charge of the international section. He did a lot of travelling, negotiating contracts with clients and suppliers. During the last five years he was with IAI, he was vice-president for marketing. At first, eyebrows were raised when he was given this appointment, but pretty soon everyone recognized that he was most suited for the job. When he retired from IAI, he wanted me to retire from my teaching job.

"Then we could travel together," he said.

"I'll wait another year," I answered, "and see if you stay retired."

He did not. An American aircraft company wanted to hire him, but that would have involved moving to the States and Tashie, the ardent Zionist, was not willing to leave Israel. He did agree to a consulting contract in marketing for three years. So he was travelling again. In the meantime, a new company was formed in Israel called ImageSat and Tashie was asked to be its CEO. He worked there for four years. After that, he did some consulting for another firm until he could not cope anymore.

Tashie was a family man. He was a loving husband, a remarkable father and later, a fabulous grandfather, though only a few of our grandchildren remember him when he was healthy. He played with the children, joked with them and produced all kinds of "shtick," which the children loved.

In 2007, in the spring, Tashie began to act depressed. He brooded and slept a lot. When I asked what was bothering him, he answered, "Nothing." I knew that it wasn't "nothing."

Then one day, he burst out, "I have the beginning of Alzheimer's."

Tashie had good reason to suspect Alzheimer's disease. His mother had had it in the last years of her life, as had her sister and her two brothers. But they had all gotten the disease in their eighties, and Tashie was only seventy years old.

We went to a psychiatrist, then a neurologist. They each reassured him that he didn't have Alzheimer's. We looked for other possible explanations for his forgetting things and repeating the same questions, but in the end, the diagnosis was Alzheimer's. It was very painful for me to watch his agony as he realized that his mind was failing him. It was not just his memory that was affected. His whole personality changed. This was no longer the man I had married and lived with for fifty years.

After ten harrowing years, Tashie contracted pneumonia and he was sent to the hospital. His condition deteriorated. On January 11, 2018, my son, David, held one of Tashie's hands and I held the other until there was a flat line on the monitor. Although I had lost him years earlier, this was final. My man was gone.

Epilogue

I had a happy childhood in Italy and in Canada. I married a wonderful man and we lived an exciting and joyful life together. I have three children — Pnina, David and Shlomit, who are all intelligent, kind, sensitive and successful in their careers. In Israel, Pnina is a successful lawyer and David works in the high-tech industry. In Toronto, Shlomit worked in a high-tech company for thirteen years; she now works for an NGO that promotes social inclusion in marginalized sectors of their communities around the world.

I love all of my children's spouses and my grandchildren. Pnina and Navot have two sons, Eitan and Ohad, who are now finding their way into adulthood. David and Carmel have a son, Yonatan, and a daughter, Mika, both of whom are now serving in the Israeli army. Shlomit and Michal have three children: Amit, who was born in 2010, and twins, Alma and Noam, who were born in 2013. All of this is my triumph over Hitler.

My parents were very grateful to Canada for accepting us and letting us live in freedom and equality with all other citizens. I took it all for granted, but my parents remembered the antisemitism that had existed in Poland even before the war, and they appreciated the security that Canada granted us.

Although most of us now live in Israel, none of us have ever severed our connection with Canada. We have relatives and friends there, and we visit Montreal and Toronto very frequently.

The chances of a four-year-old Jewish girl surviving the Holocaust in Poland were infinitesimal, yet I survived. If I believed in miracles, I would say that my survival was a miracle. Of course, a miracle needs a little help from human effort. My parents made every effort to save us all, and I believe that they were largely motivated by their love for me. I know that I am alive today thanks to their bravery, to the initiative of my uncle Shieh, to a large measure of luck and to both Klemens and the Krynski family, who sheltered us. May their names and their deeds be remembered by my descendants for many years.

Glossary

aliyah (Hebrew; pl. *aliyot*, ascent) A term used by Jews and modern Israelis to refer to Jewish immigration to Israel; the term is also used to refer to "going up" to the altar in a synagogue to read from the Torah.

British Mandate Palestine (Also Mandatory Palestine) The area of the Middle East under British rule from 1923 to 1948 comprising present-day Israel, Jordan, the West Bank and the Gaza Strip. The Mandate was established by the League of Nations after World War I and the collapse of the Ottoman Empire; the area was given to the British to administer until a Jewish national home could be established. During this time, Jewish immigration was severely restricted, and Jews and Arabs clashed with the British and each other as they struggled to realize their national interests. The Mandate ended on May 15, 1948, after the United Nations Partition Plan for Palestine was adopted and on the same day that the State of Israel was declared.

chuppah (Hebrew; canopy) The canopy used in traditional Jewish weddings that is usually made of a cloth (sometimes a prayer shawl) stretched or supported over four poles. It is meant to symbolize the home the couple will build together.

displaced persons People who find themselves homeless and stateless at the end of a war. Following World War II, millions of people, especially European Jews, found that they had no homes to return to or that it was unsafe to do so. To resolve the staggering refugee crisis that resulted, Allied authorities and the United Nations Relief and Rehabilitation Administration (UNRRA) established displaced persons (DP) camps to provide temporary shelter and assistance to refugees and help them transition toward resettlement. *See also* displaced persons (DP) camps; UNRRA.

displaced persons (DP) camps Facilities set up by the Allied authorities and the United Nations Relief and Rehabilitation Administration (UNRRA) in October 1945 to resolve the refugee crisis that arose at the end of World War II. The camps provided temporary shelter and assistance to the millions of people — not only Jews — who had been displaced from their home countries as a result of the war and helped them prepare for resettlement.

El Maleh Rachamim (Hebrew; God, full of compassion) A prayer for the soul of someone who has died, recited at funeral services, at memorial services held during the year, and to mark the anniversary of the individual's death.

ghetto A confined residential area for Jews. The term originated in Venice, Italy, in 1516 with a law requiring all Jews to live on a segregated, gated island known as Ghetto Nuovo. Throughout the Middle Ages in Europe, Jews were often forcibly confined to gated Jewish neighbourhoods. Beginning in 1939, the Nazis forced Jews to live in crowded and unsanitary conditions in designated areas — usually the poorest ones — of cities and towns in Eastern Europe. Ghettos were often enclosed by walls and gates, and entry and exit from the ghettos were strictly controlled. Family and community life continued to some degree, but starvation and disease were rampant. Starting in 1941, the ghettos were liquidated, and Jews were deported to camps and killing centres.

Habonim (Hebrew; builders) A Labour Zionist group that encouraged Jewish youth to become pioneers in Palestine and help build the Jewish homeland. It promoted activities such as camping and scouting, and educated youth in Jewish history. *See also* Labour Zionism.

Haggadah (Hebrew; telling) A book of readings that lays out the order of the Passover seder and recounts the biblical exodus from Egypt. *See also* Passover; seder.

Jewish Agency (in Hebrew, HaSochnut HaYehudit L'Eretz Yisra'el; Jewish Agency for Israel) The organization established by the World Zionist Organization in 1929 that was largely responsible for economic and cultural development of pre-state Israel, as well as immigration and supporting resettlement of immigrants. The Jewish Agency's main current function is facilitating immigration to Israel.

Jewish Brigade A battalion of approximately 5,000 volunteers from Palestine, formed in September 1944, that was under the command of the British Eighth Army and fought against the German army in Italy. After the war, the Brigade played an important role in helping Jewish refugees in Europe and organizing their entry into Palestine. The Jewish Brigade was disbanded by the British in 1946.

Judenrat (German; pl. Judenräte; Jewish Council) A group of Jewish leaders appointed by the German occupiers to administer the ghettos and carry out Nazi orders. The Judenräte tried to provide social services to the Jewish population to alleviate the harsh conditions of the ghettos and maintain a sense of community. Although the Judenräte appeared to be self-governing entities, they were actually under complete Nazi control. The Judenräte faced difficult and complex moral decisions under brutal conditions — they had to decide whether to cooperate with or resist Nazi demands, when refusal likely meant death, and they had to determine which actions might save some of the population and which might worsen their fates. The Judenräte were under extreme pressure and they remain a contentious subject.

Kaddish (Aramaic; holy. Also known as the Mourner's Kaddish or

Mourner's Prayer.) The prayer recited by mourners at funerals and memorials and during Jewish prayer services. Kaddish is traditionally said by a relative of the deceased for eleven months after the death of a parent and for thirty days after the death of a spouse or sibling, as well as each year on the anniversary of the death.

kibbutz (Hebrew) A collectively owned farm or settlement in Israel, democratically governed by its members.

Labour Zionism A secular socialist Zionist movement that promotes the building of a Jewish state through the efforts of Jewish workers. *See also* Zionism.

Organization for Rehabilitation through Training (ORT) A vocational school system founded for Jews by Jews in Russia in 1880 to promote economic self-sufficiency in impoverished communities. The name ORT derives from the acronym of the Russian organization Obshestvo Remeslenogo Zemledelcheskogo Truda, Society for Trades and Agricultural Labour. ORT schools continued to operate through World War II. After the war, ORT set up rehabilitation programs for the survivors, serving approximately 85,000 people in 78 DP camps in Germany. Today, ORT is a nonprofit organization that provides educational services to communities all over the world.

Passover (in Hebrew, Pesach) An eight-day Jewish festival (observed for seven days in Israel) that takes place in the spring and commemorates the exodus of the Israelite slaves from Egypt. The festival begins with a lavish ritual meal called a seder, during which the story of the Exodus is told through the reading of a Jewish text called the Haggadah. During Passover, Jews refrain from eating any leavened foods. The name of the festival refers to God's "passing over" the houses of the Jews and sparing their lives during the last of the ten plagues, when the first-born sons of Egyptians were killed by God. *See also* Haggadah; seder.

Polish Home Army (in Polish, Armia Krajowa) Also known as AK or the Home Army, the Polish Home Army was the largest armed resistance movement in German-occupied Poland during World War II. Although it has been criticized for antisemitism, and some factions were even guilty of killing Jews, the AK also established a Section for Jewish Affairs that collected information about what was happening to Jews in Poland, coordinated communications between Polish and Jewish resistance organizations, and supported the Council for Aid to Jews.

Purim (Hebrew; lots) The Jewish holiday that celebrates the Jews' escape from annihilation in Persia. The Purim story recounts how Haman, advisor to the King of Persia, planned to rid Persia of Jews, and how Queen Esther and her cousin Mordecai foiled Haman's plot by convincing the king to save the Jews. During the Purim festivities, people dress up as one of the figures in the Purim story, hold parades and retell the story of Haman, Esther and Mordecai.

Righteous Among the Nations A title given by Yad Vashem, the World Holocaust Remembrance Center in Jerusalem, to honour non-Jews who risked their lives to help save Jews during the Holocaust. A commission was established in 1963 to award the title. If a person fits certain criteria and the story is carefully checked, the honouree is awarded with a medal and certificate and is commemorated on the Wall of Honour at the Garden of the Righteous in Jerusalem. *See also* Yad Vashem.

Rosh Hashanah (Hebrew; New Year) The two-day autumn holiday that marks the beginning of the Jewish year and ushers in the High Holy Days. It is celebrated with a prayer service and the blowing of the shofar (ram's horn), as well as festive meals that include symbolic foods such as an apple dipped in honey, which symbolizes the desire for a sweet new year. *See also* Yom Kippur.

seder (Hebrew; order) A ritual meal celebrated at the beginning of the festival of Passover. A traditional seder involves reading the Haggadah, which tells the story of the Israelite slaves' exodus from Egypt; drinking four cups of wine; eating matzah and other symbolic foods that are arranged on a special seder plate; partaking in a festive meal; and singing traditional songs. *See also* Haggadah; Passover.

shiva (Hebrew; seven) In Judaism, the seven-day mourning period that is observed after the funeral of a close relative.

Six-Day War The armed conflict between Israel and its neighbouring states of Egypt, Jordan and Syria that took place June 5–10, 1967. In response to growing tensions between Israel and its neighbouring Arab countries, Israel launched a pre-emptive attack. In the days that followed, Israeli forces drove the Arab armies back and occupied the Sinai Peninsula, Gaza Strip, West Bank and Golan Heights. Israel also reunited Jerusalem, the eastern half of which Jordan had controlled since the 1948 Arab-Israeli war.

shtetl (Yiddish) A mostly Jewish market town in Eastern Europe before World War II. Life in the shtetl revolved around Judaism and Jewish culture and was defined by the closely intertwined economic and social lives of its residents. Shtetls existed in Eastern Europe from the sixteenth century until they were wiped out in the Holocaust.

Treblinka A Nazi death camp in German-occupied Poland about eighty kilometres northeast of Warsaw, established in 1942. Treblinka was the third death camp built specifically for the implementation of Operation Reinhard, the planned mass murder of the Jews in occupied Poland. The first massive deportations to Treblinka were from Warsaw and began on July 22, 1942. Inmates of the camp staged an uprising in August 1943 and hundreds of prisoners escaped, but the majority of them were caught and killed. Treblinka was dismantled in the fall of 1943. Approximately 900,000 Jews and unknown numbers of Poles, Roma and Soviet POWs (prisoners of war) were killed in Treblinka.

ulpan (Hebrew; pl. *ulpanim*) An intensive Hebrew-language study program for new immigrants to Israel, first established in Jerusalem in 1949. *Ulpanim* also teach Israeli culture, history and geography to help new immigrants acclimatize to life in Israel.

United Nations Relief and Rehabilitation Administration (UNRRA)
An international relief agency created at a 44-nation conference in Washington, DC, on November 9, 1943, to provide economic assistance and basic necessities to war refugees. It was especially active in repatriating and assisting refugees in the formerly Nazi-occupied European nations immediately after World War II.

World Zionist Congress The legislative body of the World Zionist Organization, first convened in 1897 by Theodor Herzl to promote the establishment of the State of Israel. Since the establishment of the State of Israel, elected delegates to the World Zionist Congress gather in Jerusalem every five years to allocate funds, assign leadership and decide on policies for major Zionist organizations in Israel and worldwide.

Yad Vashem Israel's official Holocaust memorial centre and the world's largest collection of information on the Holocaust, established in 1953. Yad Vashem, the World Holocaust Remembrance Center, is dedicated to commemoration, research, documentation and education about the Holocaust. The Yad Vashem complex in Jerusalem includes museums, sculptures, exhibitions, research centres and the Garden of the Righteous Among the Nations. *See also* Righteous Among the Nations.

Yom Kippur (Hebrew; Day of Atonement) A solemn day of fasting and repentance that comes eight days after Rosh Hashanah, the Jewish New Year, and marks the end of the High Holidays. *See also* Rosh Hashanah.

Zionism A movement promoted by the Viennese Jewish journalist Theodor Herzl, who argued in his 1896 book *Der Judenstaat* (The Jewish State) that the best way to resolve the problem of antisemitism and persecution of Jews in Europe was to create an independent Jewish state in the historical Jewish homeland of biblical Israel. Zionists also promoted the revival of Hebrew as a Jewish national language.

Photographs

Rachel Kejles during her youth. Grodzisk, Poland, age and date unknown.

1

2

3

1   Rachel Kejles before the war. Poland, date unknown.

2   Rachel in Grodzisk, Poland, November 28, 1932.

3   Rachel (standing in back, left), with family before the war. In back (right) is Rachel's sister Itke. In front (left to right): Rachel's uncle Menashe; her niece Chaya (Shieh's daughter); her mother, Rivka; her nephew Shieleh (Henia's son); and her father, Ephraim. Grodzisk, Poland, circa 1933.

1

2

1 A photo of eighteen-year-old Abraham (Avrumeh) Lisogurski on a Rosh Hashanah greeting card. Siemiatycze, Poland, October 1929.
2 The Lisogurski family in front of their house before the war. Avrumeh is standing
   in back (left) beside his father, Shmuel (right). In front (left to right): Avrumeh's
   younger brothers, Srulek and Yudel, his mother, Ruchl, and his older brother,
   Pesach. Siemiatycze, Poland, early 1930s.

1

2

1 Avrumeh and Rachel with family before they were married. From left to right:
   Avrumeh, Rachel, her sister Henia, her brother-in-law Sruleh, and a friend, name
   unknown. Siemiatycze, Poland, circa 1930s.
2 Rachel and Avrumeh (front, second and third from left) celebrating their wedding with family and friends. Warsaw, Poland, December 1937.

1 Chana Lisogurski, age eight, in the Cremona displaced persons (DP) camp after the war. Italy, 1946.
2 Chana in the Cremona DP camp. Italy, 1947.
3 Chana and Shieleh (Sidney) on a UNRRA Jeep. Italy, 1945.
4 Chana's uncle Shieh, his second wife, Halina (Hela), and their baby, Ephraim (Freddy), after the war. Warsaw, Poland, 1949.

1, 2 & 3 Passport photos of Rachel, Avrumeh and Chana Lisogurski taken in
Cremona, Italy, in preparation for their departure for Canada. May 7, 1947.

4 Chana, age ten, soon after arriving in Montreal.

1 Chana and her mother, Rachel, before Chana's wedding to Menashe (Tashie) Broder. Montreal, June 21, 1959.
2 Chana and Tashie leaving the house on their wedding day. Montreal, June 21, 1959.
3 Chana and Menashe celebrating their wedding. Montreal, June 21, 1959.

1 Chana (left, wearing a poncho crocheted by her mother), with her cousin Sidney
Zoltak and his wife, Annie. Quebec City, 1960s.

2 Rachel and Chana on a visit to Newport, Rhode Island, 1985.

1 Chana and Rachel at the wedding of Chana's eldest daughter, Pnina. Kidron, Israel, August 1992.
2 Chana and Menashe dancing at Pnina's wedding. Israel, August 1992.
3 Pnina Broder and Navot Manor on their wedding day. Kidron, Israel, August 1992.
4 David Broder and Carmel Gerstner on their wedding day. Shefayim, Israel, August 1993.

1 Shlomit Broder (right), and Michal Shahak on their wedding day. Toronto, May 2006.

2 The Broder family celebrating Chana and Tashie's fiftieth wedding anniversary. From left to right: Pnina, David, Chana, Tashie and Shlomit. Montreal, June 2009.

Chana and Tashie on the occasion of their fiftieth wedding anniversary. Montreal, 2009.

1 Chana and Tashie with their grandchildren Ohad Manor (back, left), Eitan Manor (back, right), Mika Broder (front, left) and Yonatan Broder (front, right). Tel Aviv, July 2009.

2 Chana and Tashie's grandchildren Amit, Alma and Noam. Seattle, Washington, 2019.

Chana Broder reuniting with Henryk (Heniek) Krynski, son of Konstanty and
Bronislawa Krynski, who saved Chana and her family during the war. Morze,
Poland, 1997.

1

2

3

1   Chana with Izabella Wierzbicka, granddaughter of Krysia Krynski. Izabella had researched her great-grandparents' wartime story of saving a Jewish family and located Chana, who was motivated to nominate the family for the honour of Righteous Among the Nations. Siemiatycze, Poland, May 2016.

2   Chana speaking at the Righteous Among the Nations ceremony in honour of the Krynski family. Siemiatycze, May 24, 2016.

3   Chana (centre) with Zdzislawa Chlebowska (Krysia's oldest daughter, left) accepting the award on behalf of the Krynski family, and Israeli Ambassador to Poland Anna Azari (right). Siemiatycze, May 24, 2016.

1 Chana (front, left) with her family at their first meeting with the descendants of the Krynski family at the home of Zdzislawa Chlebowska (front, right). Siemiaty-cze, May 24 2016.

2 Chana (centre) with family, descendants of the Krynski family and a group of officials at the plaque memorializing the site of the mass grave at the Jewish cemetery. Chana's grandfather's name is inscribed on the plaque. Siemiatycze, May 24, 2016.

1   Chana with her grandchildren celebrating the occasion of her eightieth birthday.
From left to right: Noam, Ohad, Amit, Eitan, Chana, Mika, Alma and Yonatan.
Galilee, Israel, December 2018.

2   Chana with her children, their partners and her grandchildren celebrating
her birthday. From left to right: Michal, Noam, Shlomit, Amit, Ohad, Eitan,
Alma, Mika, Pnina, Chana, Yonatan, David, Carmel and Navot. Galilee, Israel,
December 2018.

Index

The Azrieli Foundation was established in 1989 to realize and extend the philanthropic vision of David J. Azrieli, C.M., C.Q., M.Arch. The Foundation's mission is to support a wide spectrum of initiatives in education and research. The Azrieli Foundation is an active supporter of programs in the fields of education, the education of architects, scientific and medical research, and the arts. The Azrieli Foundation's many initiatives include: the Holocaust Survivor Memoirs Program, which collects, preserves, publishes and distributes the written memoirs of survivors in Canada; the Azrieli Institute for Educational Empowerment, an innovative program successfully working to keep at-risk youth in school; the Azrieli Fellows Program, which promotes academic excellence and leadership on the graduate level at Israeli universities; the Azrieli Music Project, which celebrates and fosters the creation of high-quality new Jewish orchestral music; and the Azrieli Neurodevelopmental Research Program, which supports advanced research on neurodevelopmental disorders, particularly Fragile X and Autism Spectrum Disorders.